At Sylvan, we believe reading is one of life's most important and enriching abilities, and we're glad you've chosen our resources to help your child build these critically important skills. We know that the time you spend with your child reinforcing the lessons learned in school will contribute to his love of reading. This love of reading will translate into academic achievement. A successful reader is ready for the world around him, ready to do research, ready to experience the world of literature, and prepared to make the connections necessary to achieve in school and in life.

We use a research-based, step-by-step process in teaching reading at Sylvan that includes thought-provoking reading selections and activities. As students increase their success as readers they become more confident. With increasing confidence, students build even more success. Our Sylvan workbooks are designed to help you to help your child build the skills and confidence that will contribute to your child's success in school.

We're excited to partner with you to support the development of a confident, well-prepared independent learner!

The Sylvan Team

Sylvan Learning Center.
Unleash your child's potential here.

No matter how big or small the academic challenge, every child has the ability to learn. But sometimes children need help making it happen. Sylvan believes every child has the potential to do great things. And we know better than anyone else how to tap into that academic potential so that a child's future really is full of possibilities. Sylvan Learning Center is the place where your child can build and master the learning skills needed to succeed and unlock the potential you know is there.

The proven, personalized approach of our in-center programs deliver unparalleled results that other supplemental education services simply can't match. Your child's achievements will be seen not only in test scores and report cards but outside the classroom as well. And when he starts achieving his full potential, everyone will know it. You will see a new level of confidence come through in everything he does and every interaction he has.

How can Sylvan's personalized in-center approach help your child unleash his potential?

• Starting with our exclusive Sylvan Skills Assessment®, we pinpoint your child's exact academic needs.

• Then we develop a customized learning plan designed to achieve your child's academic goals.

• Through our method of skill mastery, your child will not only learn and master every skill in his personalized plan, he will be truly motivated and inspired to achieve his full potential.

To get started, simply contact your local Sylvan Learning Center to set up an appointment. And to learn more about Sylvan and our innovative in-center programs, call 1-800-EDUCATE or visit www.SylvanLearning.com. *With over 850 locations in North America, there is a Sylvan Learning Center near you!*

1st Grade
Jumbo Language Arts Success
Workbook

Copyright © 2009 by Sylvan Learning, Inc.

Published in the United States by Random House, Inc., New York, and in Canada by Random House of Canada Limited, Toronto.

This book was previously published with the title *1st Grade Language Arts Success* as a trade paperback by Sylvan Learning, Inc., an imprint of Penguin Random House LLC, in 2009.

www.sylvanlearning.com

Created by Smarterville Productions LLC
Producer: TJ Trochlil McGreevy
Producer & Editorial Direction: The Linguistic Edge
Writers: Christina Roll, (Reading Skill Builders), Sandy Damashek (Spelling Games & Activities), Margaret Crocker (Vocabulary Puzzles)
Cover and Interior Illustrations: Duendes del Sur
Layout and Art Direction: SunDried Penguin
Art Manager: Adina Ficano

First Edition

ISBN: 978-0-375-43030-5

Library of Congress Cataloging-in-Publication Data available upon request.

This book is available at special discounts for bulk purchases for sales promotions or premiums.
For more information, write to Special Markets/Premium Sales, 1745 Broadway, MD 6-2,
New York, New York 10019 or e-mail specialmarkets@randomhouse.com.

PRINTED IN CHINA

12

Reading Skill Builders Contents

Spelling Games & Activities Contents

Vocabulary Puzzles Contents

1st Grade
Reading Skill Builders

Beginning Sounds

Starting Line

SAY the name of each picture and LISTEN to its beginning sound. WRITE the letter to complete each word. Then READ each word out loud.

1. bike
2. bed
3. fish
4. goat
5. dog
6. desk
7. bus
8. fork
9. doll
10. gum

Maze Crazy!

Help the bee get to the hive. DRAW a line through the maze to connect the pictures whose names begin with the **b**, **d**, or **f** sound.

Start

End

Beginning Sounds

Sounds and Words

SAY the name of the picture in each row and LISTEN to its beginning sound. CIRCLE the word or words in the row that have the same beginning sound.

1. quick   quit   fun

2. jeans   gum   jam

3. kite   kick   goat

4. mop   fan   hand

5. gas   keep   zip

What's My Word?

SAY the name of each picture. CIRCLE the word that matches the picture.

1.

hand   jam

2.

rang   king

3.

queen   nail

4.

jump   jar

5.

kite   tent

6.

girl   quilt

7.

hat   fall

8.

jug   key

Beginning Sounds

What Starts My Name?

SAY the name of each picture. WRITE the correct word for each picture under the letter that makes its beginning sound. LOOK at the word box for help.

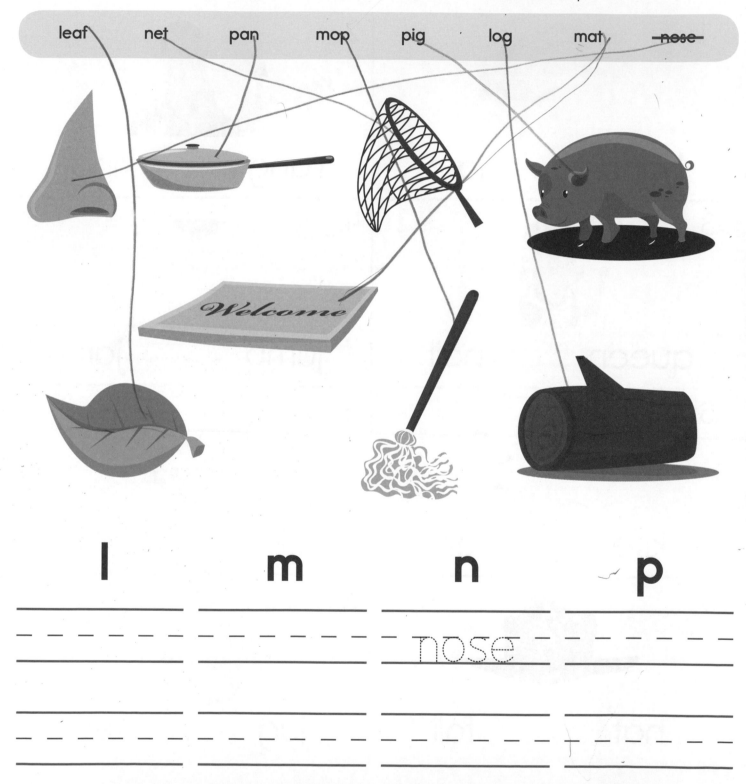

leaf   net   pan   mop   pig   log   mat   ~~nose~~

l   m   n   p

_____   _____   nose   _____

6

Picture Match

READ each sentence and FIND the matching picture. WRITE the correct number in the box.

1. I see a ladybug on a leaf.

2. The milk is on the mat.

3. The nest is next to the net.

4. I ate pizza and pie for lunch.

Beginning Sounds

Starting Line

SAY the name of each picture and LISTEN to its beginning sound. WRITE the letter to complete each word. Then READ each word out loud.

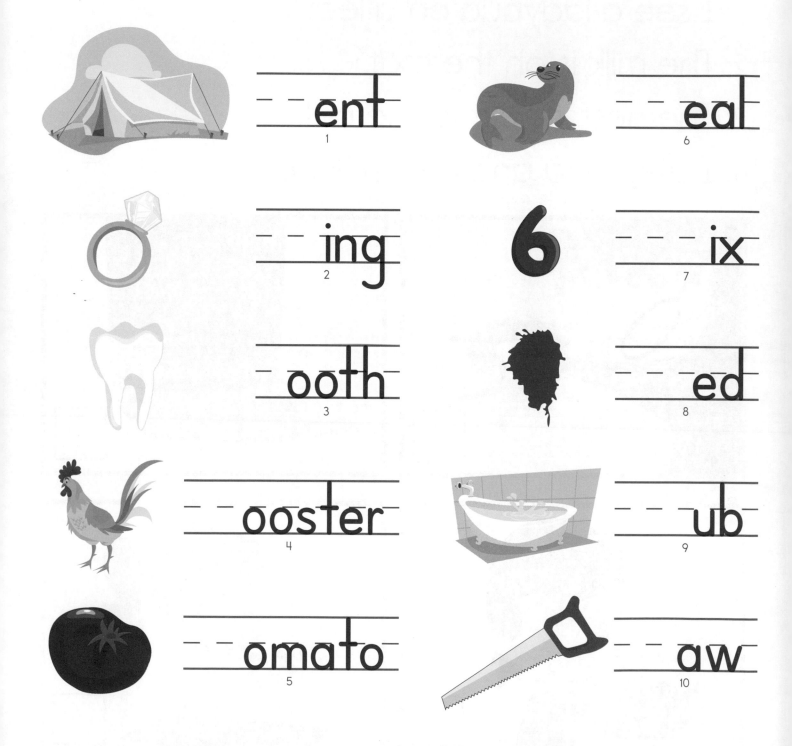

_ent
1

_ing
2

_ooth
3

_ooster
4

_omato
5

_eal
6

_ix
7

_ed
8

_ub
9

_aw
10

Double Cross

SAY the name of each picture and LISTEN to its beginning sound. DRAW a line from each picture to its name.

rake

sun

rose

tape

tooth

sink

top

rock

tie

sock

rug

seal

Beginning Sounds

What Starts My Name?

SAY the name of each picture. WRITE the correct word for each picture under the letter that makes its beginning sound. LOOK at the word box for help.

| zipper | van | wig | yo-yo | web | yellow | vase | zebra |

V

W

y

z

Word Connection

SAY the name of the picture. CIRCLE the letters that make its name. WRITE the word. Then READ the word out loud.

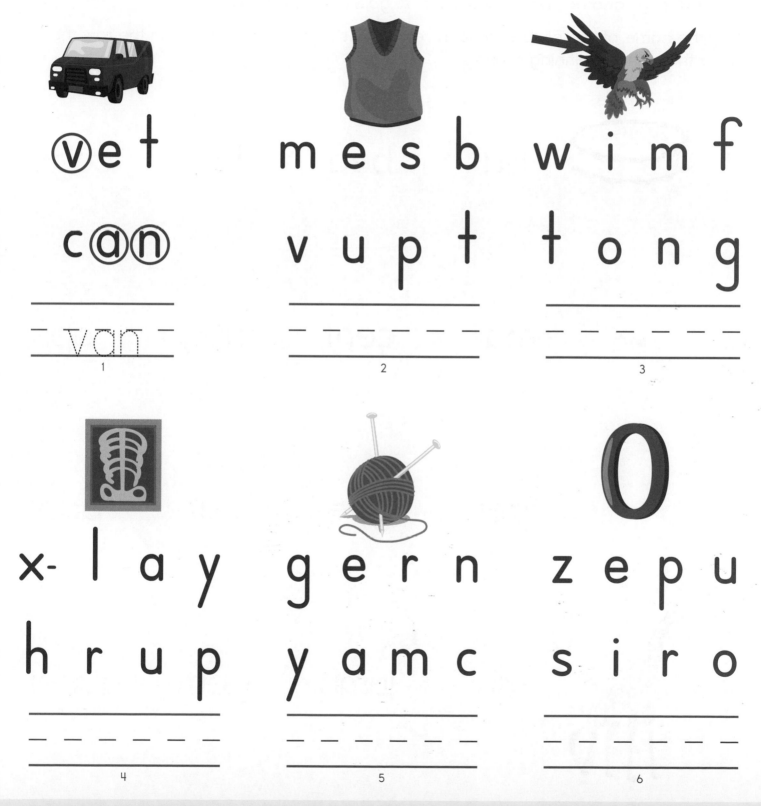

v e t

c a n

van

1

m e s b

v u p t

_____

2

w i m f

t o n g

_____

3

x- l a y

h r u p

_____

4

g e r n

y a m c

_____

5

z e p u

s i r o

_____

6

Circle It

The letter "c" has two sounds: **k** as in *coat* and **s** as in *city*.

The letter "g" also has two sounds: **g** as in *gold* and **j** as in *giant*.

SAY the name of the picture in each row. CIRCLE the word or words in the row that have the same beginning sound.

1.   kid   bed   hat   cage

2.   mail   cent   dog   sip

3.   get   give   nut   pop

4.   fish   jump   gem   queen

Picture Match

READ each sentence and FIND the matching picture. WRITE the correct number in the box.

1. The cat and cow are in the garden.
2. Look at that giant cake!
3. The goat ate corn and carrots.
4. A girl took a cab to the city.

Ending Sounds

Finish Line

SAY the name of each picture and LISTEN to its ending sound. WRITE the letter to complete each word. Then READ each word out loud.

re
1

su
2

mo
3

dru
4

fa
5

han
6

cri
7

ra
8

to
9

moo
10

Circle It

SAY the name of the picture in each row. CIRCLE the word or words in the row that have the same ending sound.

1. gum bird clam

2. seed moon log

3. food sad wig

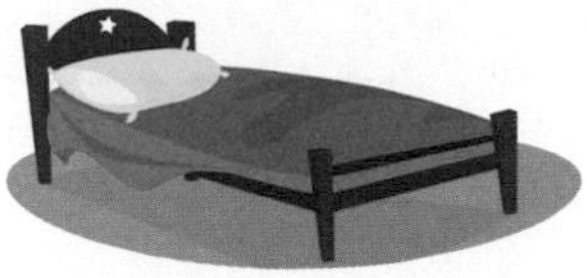

4. jump hook top

5. fix rub jet

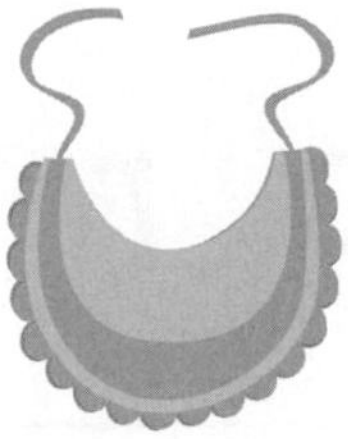

Word Connection

SAY the name of the picture. CIRCLE the letters that make its name. WRITE the word. Then READ the word out loud.

g e a k
b o e t

_____
_ _ _ _ _
_____
1

b a s l
f e l s

_____
_ _ _ _ _
_____
2

s h a g
f l i p

_____
_ _ _ _ _
_____
3

p r e t t
d l a s s

_____
_ _ _ _ _
_____
4

f a t n
b o r k

_____
_ _ _ _ _
_____
5

Double Cross

SAY the name of each picture and LISTEN to its ending sound. DRAW a line from each picture to its name.

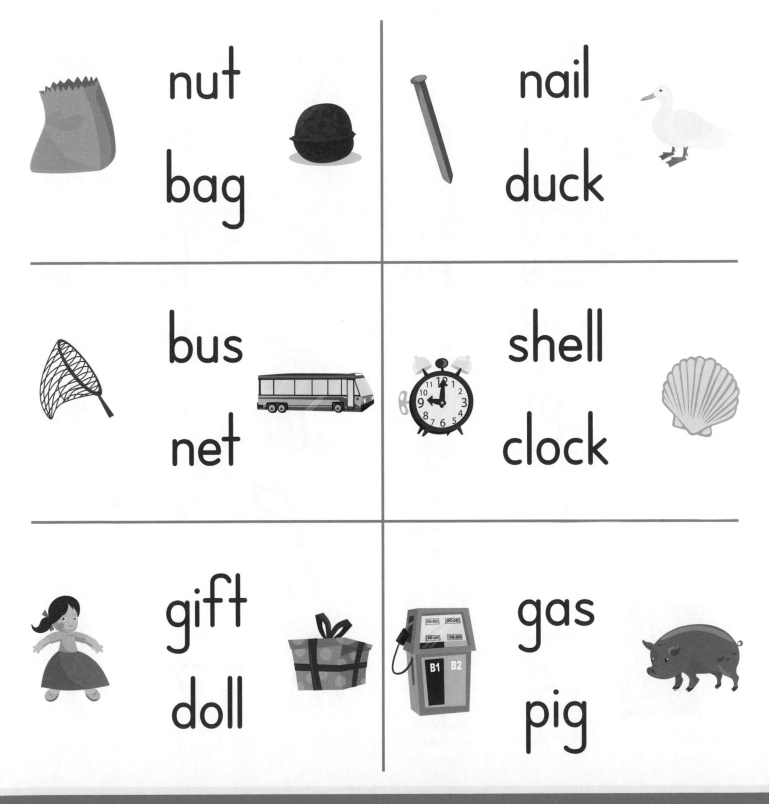

nut

bag

nail

duck

bus

net

shell

clock

gift

doll

gas

pig

Middle Sounds

Stuck in the Middle

SAY the name of each picture and LISTEN to its middle sound. WRITE the letter or letters to complete each word. Then READ each word out loud.

HINT: You may need to add more than one letter to some words.

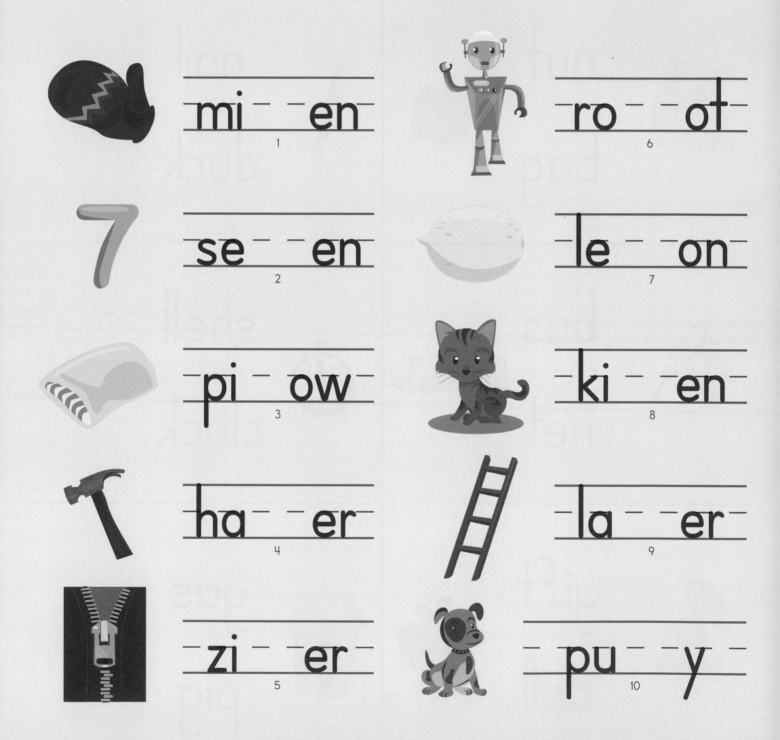

mi __ en
1

ro __ ot
6

se __ en
2

le __ on
7

pi __ ow
3

ki __ en
8

ha __ er
4

la __ er
9

zi __ er
5

pu __ y
10

Circle It

SAY the name of the picture in each row and LISTEN to its middle sound. CIRCLE the word or words in the row that have the same middle sound.

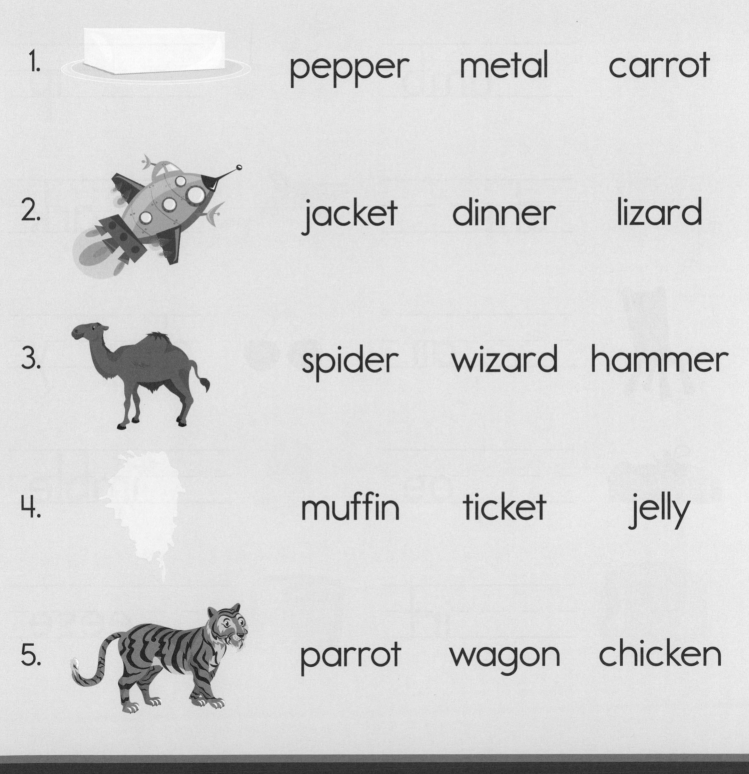

1. pepper   metal   carrot

2. jacket   dinner   lizard

3. spider   wizard   hammer

4. muffin   ticket   jelly

5. parrot   wagon   chicken

Two Letters, One Sound!

Starting Line

SAY the name of each picture and LISTEN to its beginning sound. WRITE the letters to complete each word. Then READ each word out loud.

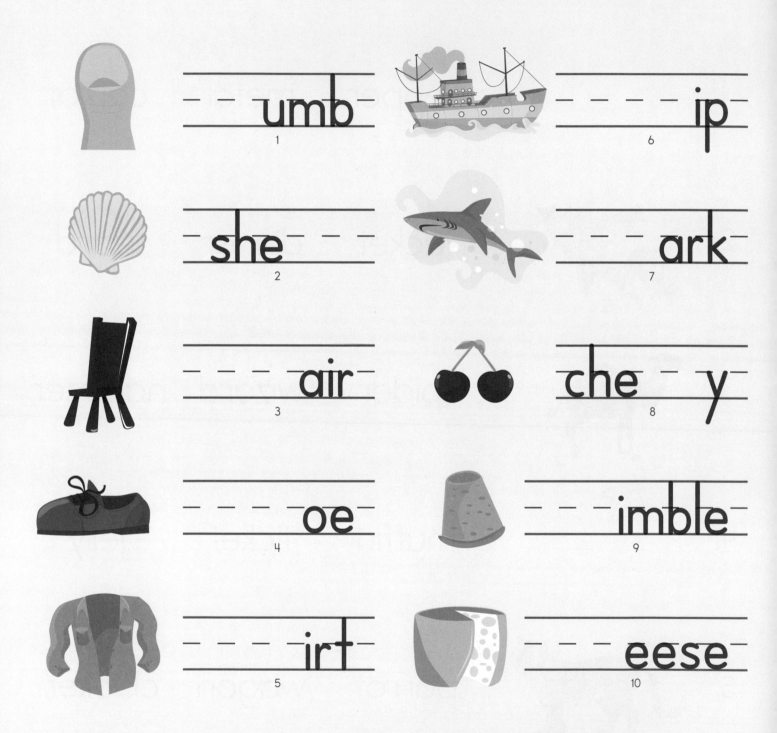

1. _ _ _ umb
2. _ _ _ she
3. _ _ _ air
4. _ _ _ oe
5. _ _ _ irt
6. _ _ _ ip
7. _ _ _ ark
8. _ _ _ che _ y
9. _ _ _ imble
10. _ _ _ eese

Blank Out

READ each sentence and LOOK at the picture. WRITE the word to complete the sentence. LOOK at the word box for help.

brush	beach	splash	moth	bench

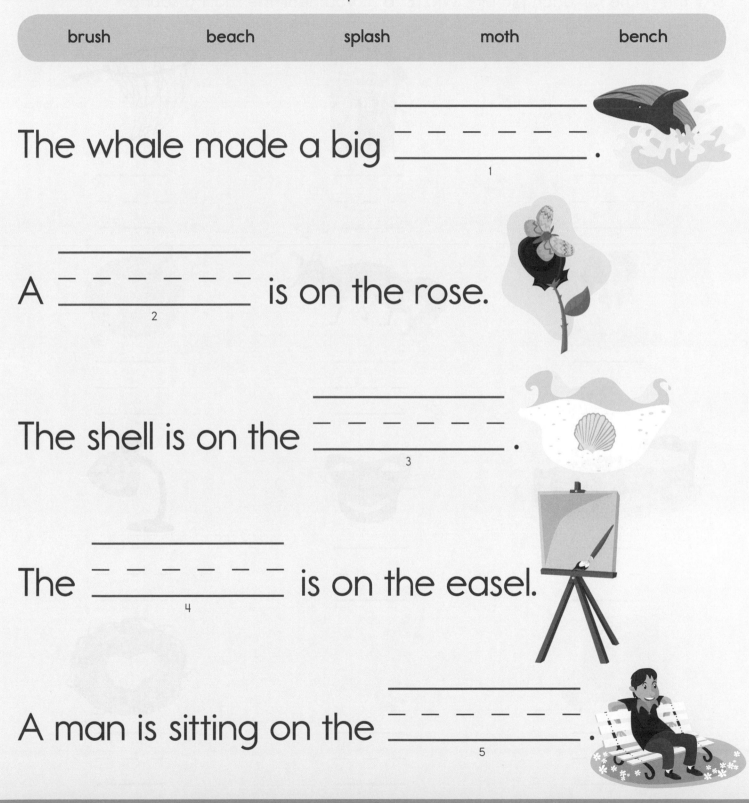

The whale made a big _____ .
1

A _____ is on the rose.
2

The shell is on the _____ .
3

The _____ is on the easel.
4

A man is sitting on the _____ .
5

Short Vowels

Same Sound

The word *hat* has a short **a** in the middle.

SAY the name for each picture. WRITE "a" if you hear the short **a** sound.

Maze Crazy!

Help the ram find the flag. DRAW a line through the maze to connect the pictures whose names have the short **a** sound.

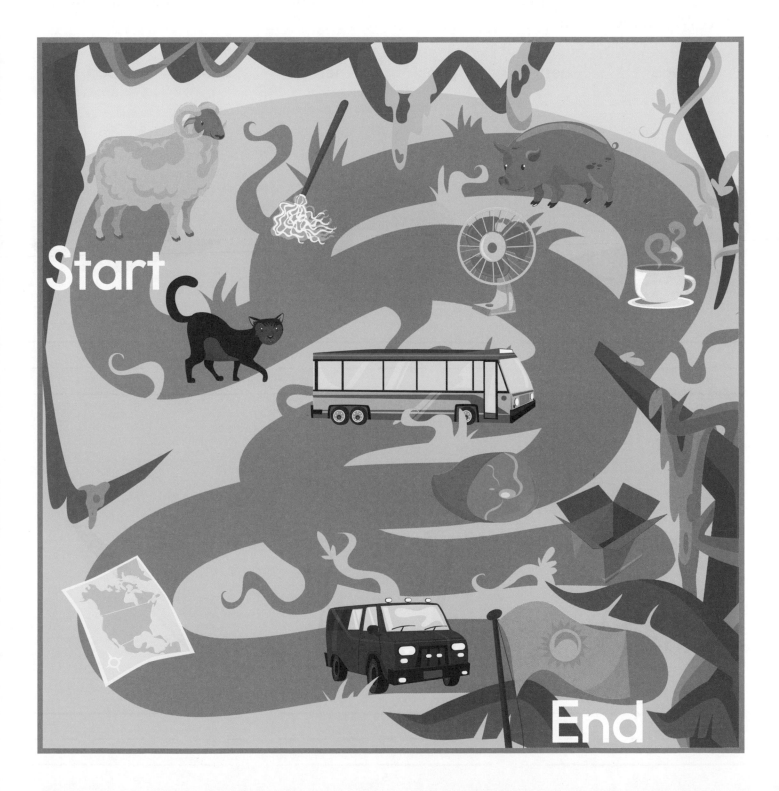

Short Vowels

Match and Write

The word *hen* has a short **e** in the middle.

SAY the name for each picture. FIND the correct name in the word box and CIRCLE it. Then WRITE the word.

| web | nest | pen | net | sled | bed |

_____
- - - - - - - - - - -
_____
1

_____
- - - - - - - - - - -
_____
2

_____
- - - - - - - - - - -
_____
3

_____
- - - - - - - - - - -
_____
4

_____
- - - - - - - - - - -
_____
5

_____
- - - - - - - - - - -
_____
6

What Am I?

WRITE the answers in the blanks. The words have the same vowel sound as in the word *hen*.

I am a bird's home.

_____
- - - - - - -
_____
1

I am what a
hen lays.

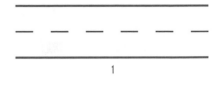

_____
- - - - - - -
_____
2

I am the number that
comes after nine.

10

_____
- - - - - - -
_____
3

I am what a spider
spins.

_____
- - - - - - -
_____
4

I am what you
sleep in.

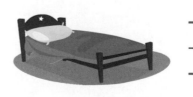

_____
- - - - - - -
_____
5

Short Vowels

Match Up

The word *wig* has a short **i** in the middle.

READ and TRACE each word. DRAW a line from the word to its matching picture.

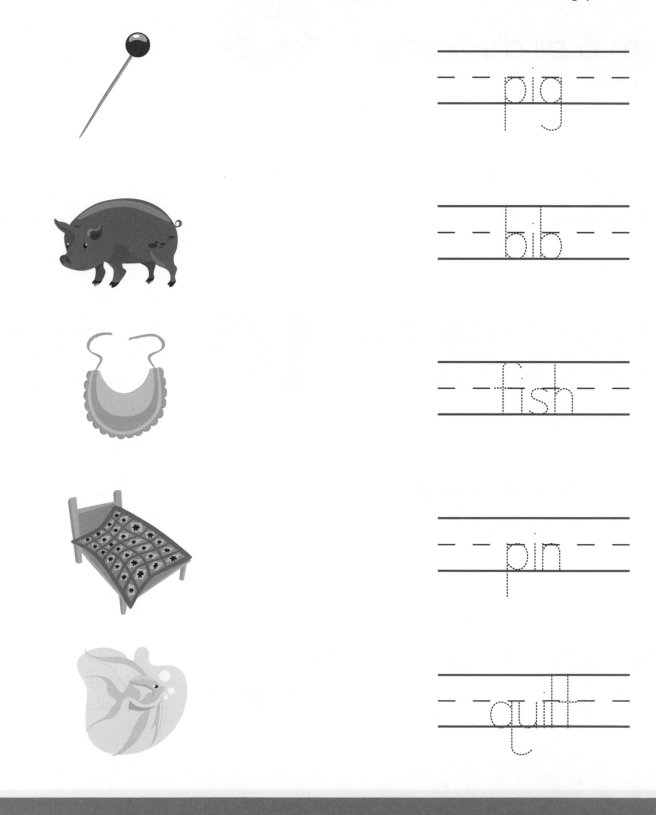

pig

bib

fish

pin

quilt

Time to Rhyme

SAY the name of each picture. CIRCLE the word or words that rhyme.

1.   hush   dish   wish

2.   pat   map   pit

3.   bib   sip   let

4.   big   peg   wig

5.   sit   mix   sack

Short Vowels

Same Sound

The word *dog* has a short **o** in the middle.

SAY the name for each picture. WRITE "o" if you hear the short **o** sound.

Maze Crazy!

Help the frog leap to the rock. DRAW a line through the maze to connect the pictures whose names have the short **o** sound.

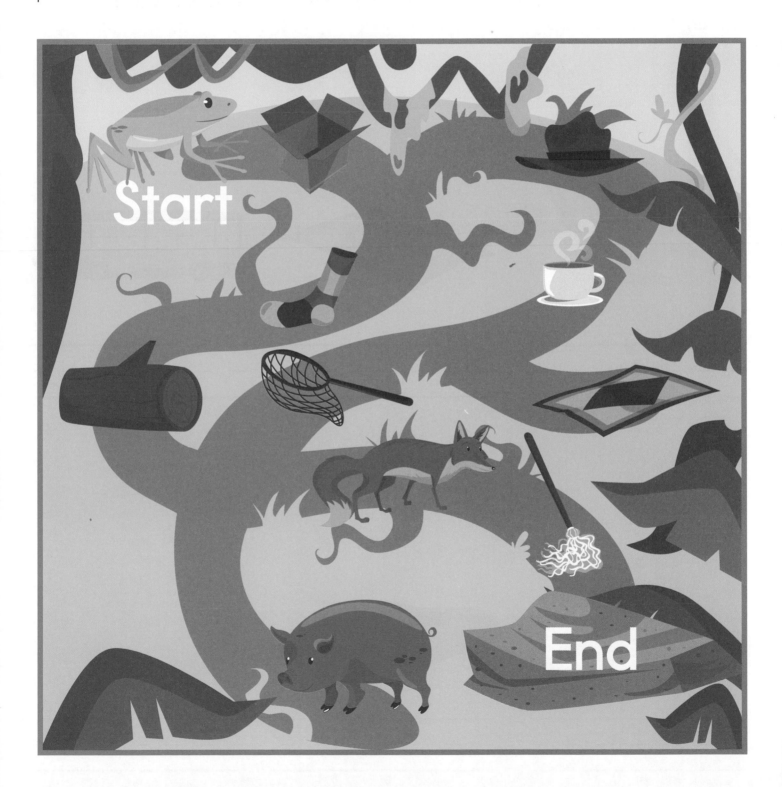

Short Vowels

Match and Write

The word *cup* has a short **u** sound in the middle.

SAY the name for each picture. FIND the correct name in the word box and CIRCLE it. Then WRITE the word.

bus	mud	tub	plug	sun	rug

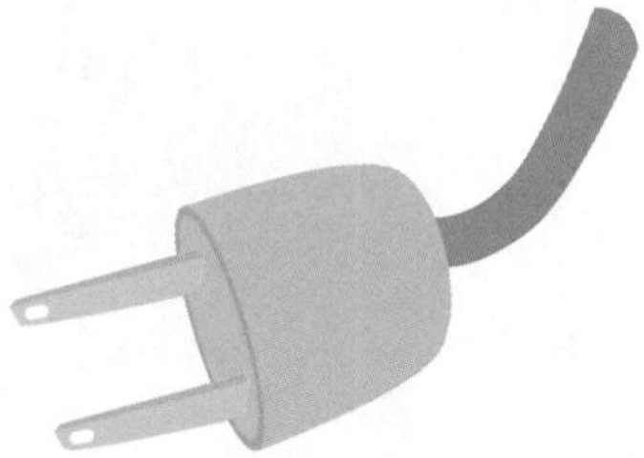

1

2

3

4

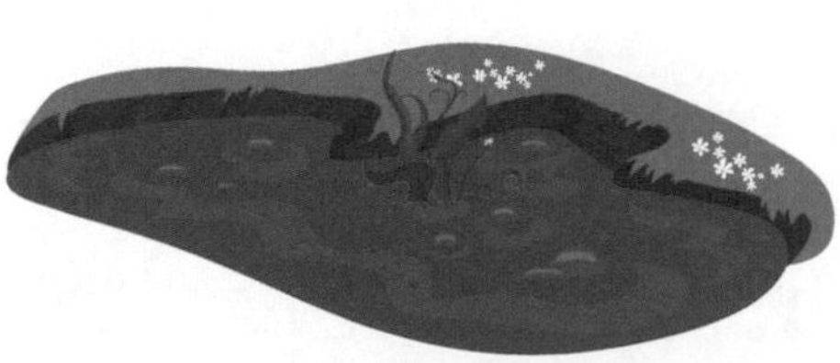

5

6

Blank Out

READ each sentence. LOOK at the picture. WRITE the word to complete the sentence. LOOK at the word box for help.

| cup | sub | gum | rug | truck |

The bug is on the _____.
1

The pup is as small as a _____.
2

The _____ is in the sun.
3

It's fun to chew _____.
4

The _____ is stuck in the mud.
5

Long Vowels

Same Sound

The word *vase* has a long **a** sound in the middle.

SAY the name for each picture. WRITE "a" if you hear the long **a** sound.

Maze Crazy!

Help the snake get to the gate. DRAW a line through the maze, connecting the pictures whose names have the long **a** sound.

Match and Write

The word *three* has a long **e** sound at the end.

SAY the name of the picture. FIND the correct name in the word box and CIRCLE it. Then WRITE the word.

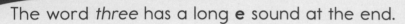

| knee | bee | sheep | green | tree | queen |

What Am I?

WRITE the answers in the blanks. The words have the same vowel sound as the word *peel*.

I can make honey.

_____

- - - - -

_____

1

I am the color of trees and grass.

_____

- - - - -

_____

2

I can go around and around.

_____

- - - - -

_____

3

I come after two and before four.

_____

- - - - -

_____

4

I am part of a shoe.

_____

- - - - -

_____

5

Match Up

The word *mice* has a long **i** sound in the middle.

READ and TRACE each word. DRAW a line from the word to its matching picture.

kite

nine

slide

tie

bike

Time to Rhyme

SAY the name of each picture. CIRCLE the word or words that rhyme.

1.   bite   cube   rope

2.   hive   save   keep

3.   pole   pave   tie

4.   wipe   ripe   dive

5.   cone   fine   dine

Long Vowels

Same Sound

The word *rose* has a long **o** in the middle.

SAY the name for each picture. WRITE "o" if you hear the long **o** sound.

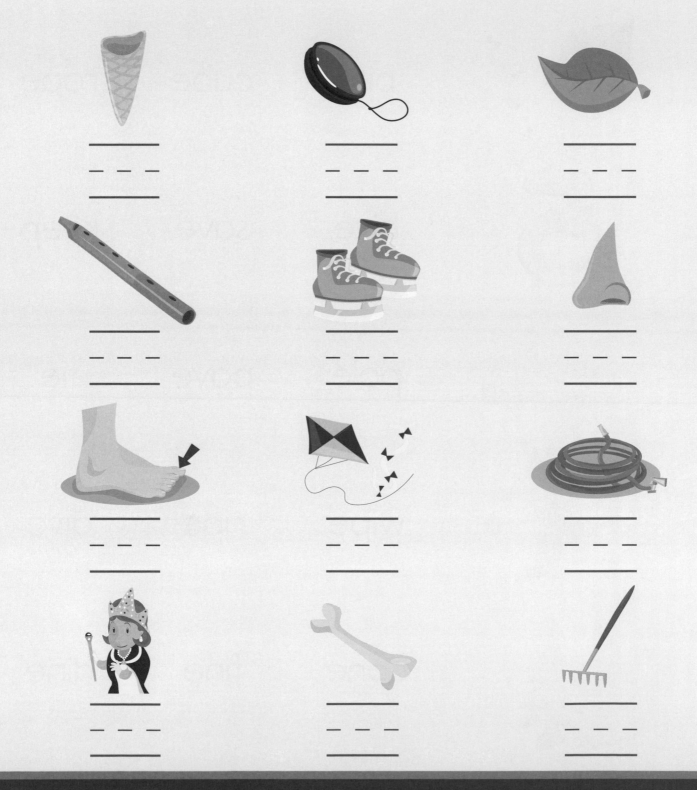

Maze Crazy!

Help the goat get to the boat. DRAW a line through the maze to connect the pictures whose names have the long **o** sound.

Long Vowels

Match and Write

Hear the long **u** sound in the word *tune*.

SAY the name of the picture. FIND the picture name in the word box and CIRCLE it.
Then WRITE the word.

flute	blue	mule	glue	tube	cube

1

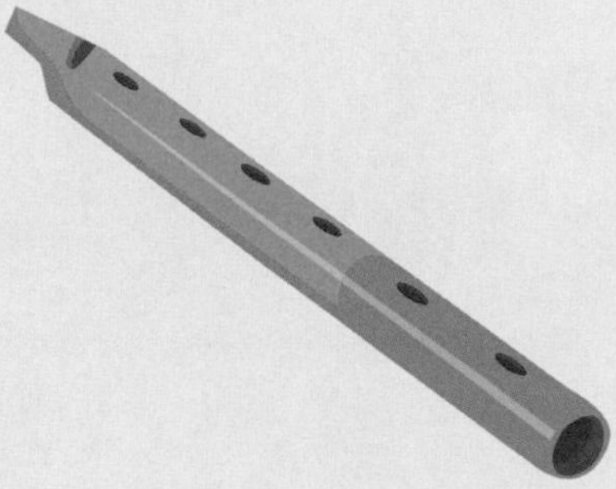

2

3

4

5

6

Blank Out

READ each sentence and LOOK at the picture. WRITE the word to complete the sentence. LOOK at the word box for help.

mule	flute	blue	glue	cube

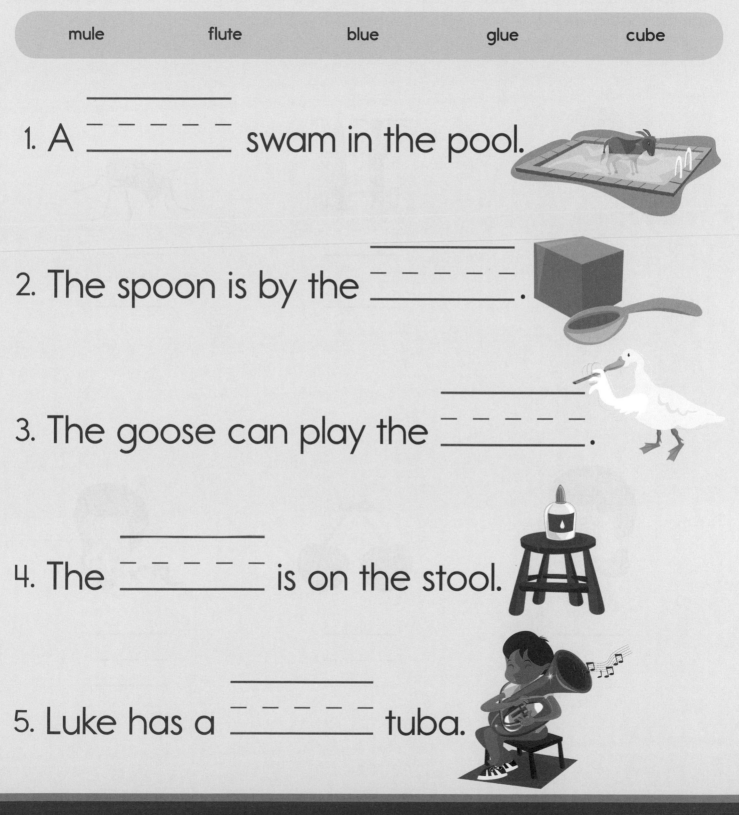

1. A _____ swam in the pool.

2. The spoon is by the _____.

3. The goose can play the _____.

4. The _____ is on the stool.

5. Luke has a _____ tuba.

Same Sound

The letter "y" can have two sounds: a long **i** sound as in *cry* or a long **e** sound as in *baby*.

SAY the name for each picture. WRITE "i" if you hear the long **i** sound and "e" if you hear the long **e** sound.

What Am I?

WRITE the answers in the blanks. The words have the long **i** or long **e** sound.

I sometimes do this in a pan.

_____

1

I am the month after June.

_____

2

I am made up of many buildings.

_____

3

I sometimes take your teeth.

_____

4

I am round and red and grow.

_____

5

Compound Words

It Takes Two

A COMPOUND word is made of two words. The two words are put together to make a new word.

WRITE the compound word made from each pair of pictures.

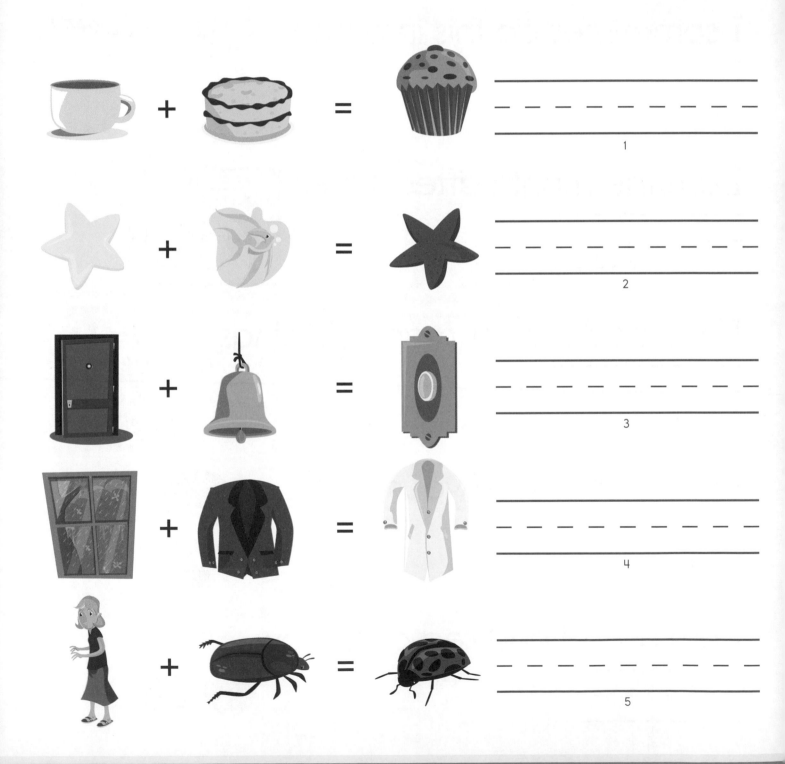

One Plus One Makes Two

LOOK at the pictures. READ the words in the word box. WRITE the compound word that matches each pair of pictures.

| football | doghouse | snowman | rainbow | catfish |

 +  = _____
1

+ = _____
2

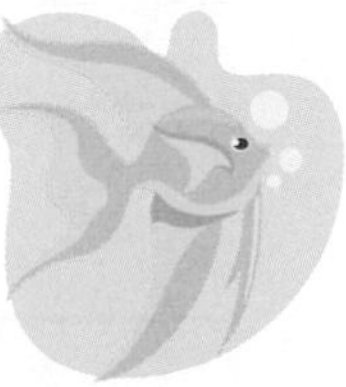

+ = _____
3

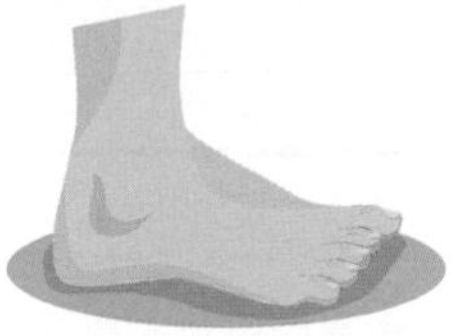

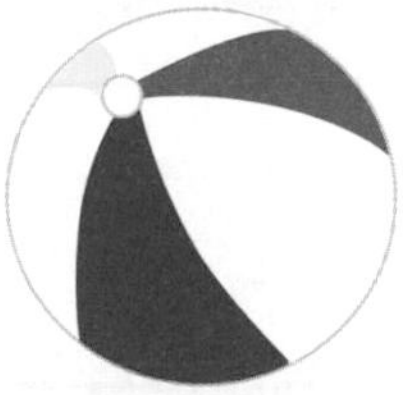

+ = _____
4

+ = _____
5

Compound Words

Put It Together

DRAW a line between the two words in each column that make a compound word. WRITE the compound word.

sail	shell	_____ _ _ _ _ _ _ _ _ _ _____ 1
bed	cake	_____ _ _ _ _ _ _ _ _ _ _____ 2
pan	box	_____ _ _ _ _ _ _ _ _ _ _____ 3
sand	boat	_____ _ _ _ _ _ _ _ _ _ _____ 4
sea	room	_____ _ _ _ _ _ _ _ _ _ _____ 5
pea	ship	_____ _ _ _ _ _ _ _ _ _ _____ 6
space	nut	_____ _ _ _ _ _ _ _ _ _ _____ 7

Word Pairs

CIRCLE the compound word in each sentence. WRITE the compound word and the two smaller words that it came from.

1. Kim and I played in the backyard.

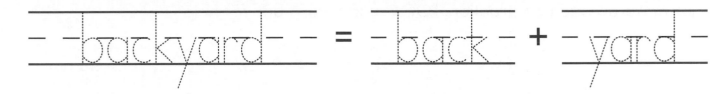

    backyard = back + yard

2. My brother likes to play baseball.

_____ = _____ + _____

3. A butterfly is on the flower.

_____ = _____ + _____

4. Kate's books are in her backpack.

_____ = _____ + _____

5. Three goldfish are in the tank.

_____ = _____ + _____

Contraction Action

One Plus One Makes...One?

A **contraction** is a shortened form of two words. A symbol called an *apostrophe* takes the place of the missing letter or letters.

Examples: is + not = isn't   he + is = he's

READ the sentences. CIRCLE the contraction in each sentence. WRITE the two words that make up each contraction. LOOK at the word box for help.

it is	I will	I am	we are	were not

1. I'll help make the bed.   _____ _____

2. I am happy that we're going to the park.   _____ _____

3. Do you think it's going to rain today?   _____ _____

4. The birds weren't in the nest.   _____ _____

5. I'm in the first grade.   _____ _____

It's a Match

DRAW a line from each contraction to the words it came from.

I'll	were not
won't	you will
I'm	I will
it's	will not
weren't	it is
you'll	cannot
they're	do not
don't	they are
can't	I am

Double the Fun

When a word has two syllables with **double** consonants in the middle, such as *rabbit*, divide the word between the consonants: *rab | bit*.

DIVIDE the words into syllables. Then WRITE the syllables next to the words.

1. din|ner   din   ner

2. kitten

3. mitten

4. happen

5. puppet

6. zipper

7. muffin

8. button

Put It Together

LOOK at each picture and the syllable next to it. FILL IN the rest of each word with a syllable from the word box.

low	za	ten	mer	ple	py

1.  ap ___ple___

2. 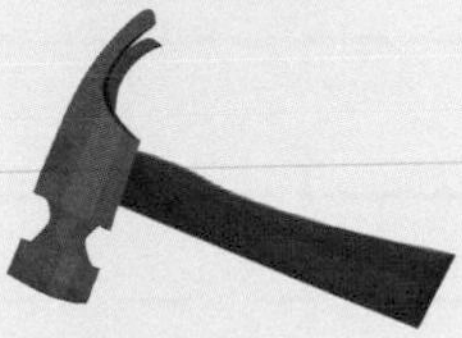 ham _____

3.  mit _____

4.  piz _____

5.  pup _____

6. yel _____

Syllables

Split It Up

When a word has two syllables with **any two consonants** in the middle, you can usually divide the word between the consonants.

DIVIDE the words into syllables. Then WRITE the syllables next to the words.

1. nap|kin   _nap_   _kin_

2. basket   _____   _____

3. doctor   _____   _____

4. picnic   _____   _____

5. monkey   _____   _____

6. winter   _____   _____

7. sister   _____   _____

8. pencil   _____   _____

Put It Together

SAY the name for each animal. FILL IN the rest of each word with a syllable from the word box.

pen	wal	mon	tur	tur	roos

1.  _____ rus

2.  _____ key

3.  _____ tle

4.  _____ ter

5.  _____ key

6.  _____ guin

Plurals

More than One

A word is **singular** when it names one person, place, or thing. A word is **plural** when it names more than one person, place, or thing. An "-s" at the end of a word often means there is more than one.

LOOK at each picture. CIRCLE the word that means the same thing as the picture. WRITE the word.

1. cat   cats

2. kite   kites

3. drum   drums

4. rose   roses

5. cake   cakes

6. frog   frogs

Make It More

READ each sentence. LOOK at the underlined word in the sentence. WRITE the plural of the word on the line.

1. They gave her a <u>gift</u>.   _____

2. That <u>map</u> is old.   _____

3. Kim is flying a <u>kite</u>.   _____

4. I read that <u>book</u>.   _____

5. The <u>cup</u> is in the sink.   _____

6. The <u>dog</u> is barking.   _____

7. I see a <u>bird</u> in the nest.   _____

8. My aunt baked a <u>cake</u>.   _____

Alternate Endings

Add "-s" to make most words plural. Add "-es" if the word ends in "sh," "ch," "tch," "s," or "x."

LOOK at the pictures. TRACE the words. ADD "-s" or "-es" to make the words plural.

dress
1

bus
2

brush
3

lamp
4

bike
5

cube
6

box
7

peach
8

Alternate Endings

Usually, when a word ends in "f," we change it to "v" and add "-es" to make the word plural.

LOOK at each picture. CIRCLE the word that means the same thing as the picture. WRITE the word.

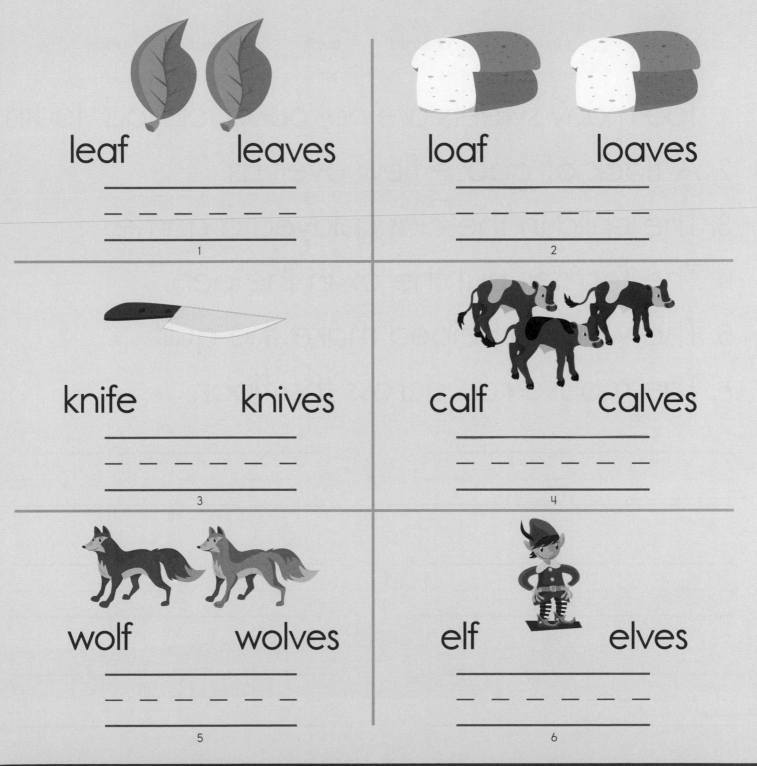

leaf   leaves

_____
- - - - - - - - - -
_____
1

loaf   loaves

_____
- - - - - - - - - -
_____
2

knife   knives

_____
- - - - - - - - - -
_____
3

calf   calves

_____
- - - - - - - - - -
_____
4

wolf   wolves

_____
- - - - - - - - - -
_____
5

elf   elves

_____
- - - - - - - - - -
_____
6

More Ways than One

Not all plurals end in "-s" or "-es." For example, the plural of *foot* is *feet*.

READ each sentence and CHANGE the word in **purple** to plural. WRITE the plural words on the numbered lines. USE the words in the word box.

women	oxen	children	teeth	geese	mice

1. Too many sweets are not good for your tooth.

2. A flock of goose flew over us.

3. The child in the class played a game.

4. The farmer put the ox in the pen.

5. The woman helped make the quilt.

6. The mouse ran across the floor.

_____   _____
_ _ _ _ _ _ _ _ _ _ _ _   _ _ _ _ _ _ _ _ _ _ _ _
_____   _____
          1   2

_____   _____
_ _ _ _ _ _ _ _ _ _ _ _   _ _ _ _ _ _ _ _ _ _ _ _
_____   _____
          3   4

_____   _____
_ _ _ _ _ _ _ _ _ _ _ _   _ _ _ _ _ _ _ _ _ _ _ _
_____   _____
          5   6

More Ways than One

MAKE these words plural.

foot _____ 1

tooth _____ 2

child _____ 3

goose _____ 4

man _____ 5

MAKE these words singular.

oxen _____ 6

firemen _____ 7

people _____ 8

mice _____ 9

women _____ 10

Words to Know

Word Blocks

FIND the word from the word box that completes each sentence. WRITE it in the blocks. USE each word only once.

old	just	four	round	sleep	fly

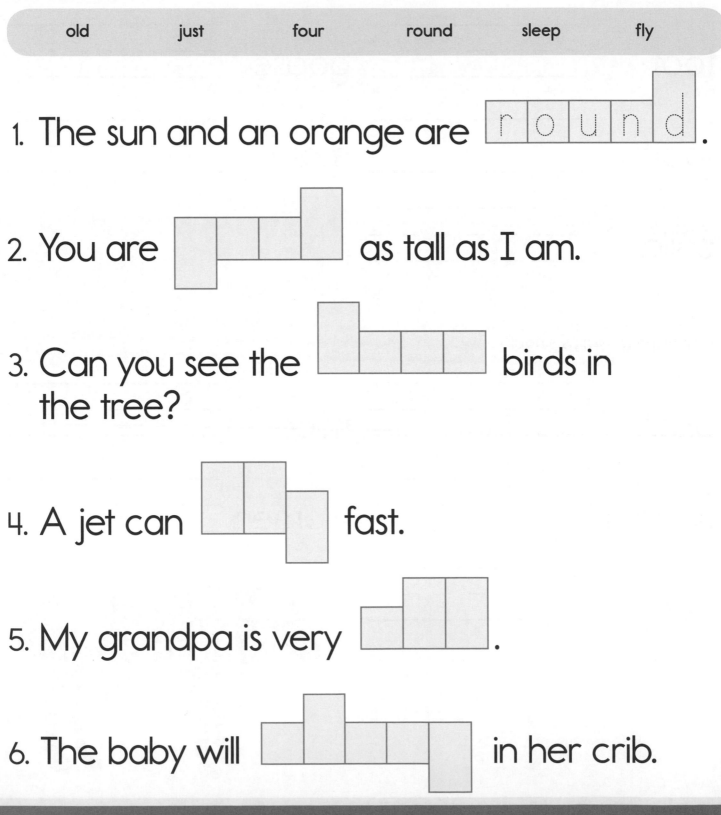

1. The sun and an orange are r o u n d .

2. You are ☐☐☐☐ as tall as I am.

3. Can you see the ☐☐☐☐ birds in the tree?

4. A jet can ☐☐☐ fast.

5. My grandpa is very ☐☐☐ .

6. The baby will ☐☐☐☐☐ in her crib.

Riddle Me This

READ each riddle. CHOOSE a word from the word box to solve the riddle. WRITE it next to each riddle.

| old | just | four | round | sleep | fly |

1. I am what a bird can do. _____

2. I come after three and before five. _____

3. I am the opposite of young. _____

4. I am what you do when you are in bed. _____

5. I am the shape of a ball. _____

6. I rhyme with the word *must*. _____

Words to Know

Match Up

READ each phrase and then MATCH it to the correct picture.

1. very old

2. went to sleep

3. just think

4. four of them

5. is round

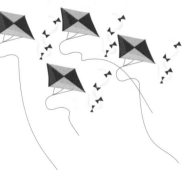

6. can fly

The Right Word

READ the words under each sentence. USE one of the words to complete the sentence.

1. Did you see the bee _____ to its hive?

   | ask | fly | think |

2. I ate _____ carrots with dinner.

   | four | sleep | after |

3. A tire and a circle are _____ .

   | some | every | round |

4. Mom said, "Please take _____ one."

   | just | with | again |

5. That _____ woman is my great aunt.

   | just | right | old |

Word Blocks

FIND the word from the word box that completes each sentence. WRITE it in the blocks. USE each word only once.

over	stop	give	sing	open	green

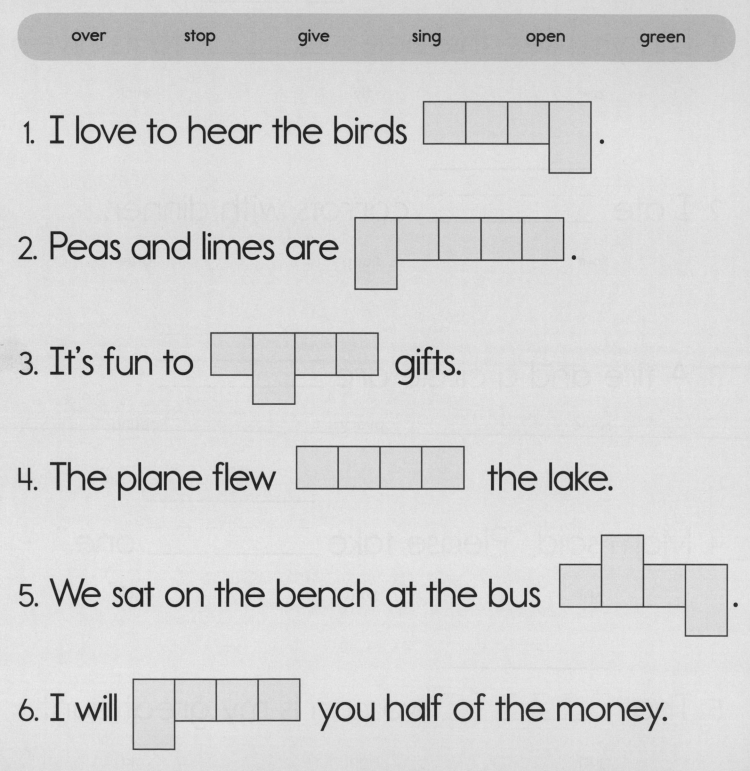

1. I love to hear the birds ⬜⬜⬜⬜ .

2. Peas and limes are ⬜⬜⬜⬜⬜ .

3. It's fun to ⬜⬜⬜⬜ gifts.

4. The plane flew ⬜⬜⬜⬜ the lake.

5. We sat on the bench at the bus ⬜⬜⬜⬜ .

6. I will ⬜⬜⬜⬜ you half of the money.

Riddle Me This

READ each riddle. CHOOSE a word from the word box to solve the riddle. WRITE it next to each riddle.

over	stop	give	open	green

1. I am the color of grass and trees. _____

2. I am the opposite of *closed*. _____

3. I rhyme with the word *clover*. _____

4. I am what you do at a red light. _____

5. I am the opposite of *take*. _____

Match Up

READ each phrase and then MATCH it to the correct picture.

1. they can sing

2. please stop

3. over there

4. will give

5. it is green

6. is open

The Right Word

READ the words under each sentence. USE one of the words to complete the sentence.

1. You should _____ and look both ways before you cross the street.

know	take	stop

2. I will _____ you a gift for your birthday.

like	give	write

3. The dog pushed the door _____ .

open	what	after

4. I love to hear the children _____ that song.

sing	put	take

5. Blue and yellow make _____ .

some	round	green

Stack Up

LOOK at the words and pictures. WRITE the names of the pictures in the correct columns.

lemon

corn

apple

carrot

orange

grapes

broccoli

lettuce

Fruits

Vegetables

_____

_____

_____

_____

_____

_____

_____

_____

_____

_____

Odd Word Out

CIRCLE the picture in each row that does **not** go with the others.

1.

cookies   cupcake   olive   pie

2.

ladybug   butterfly   dog   bee

3.

yarn   pants   dress   shirt

WRITE the names of the pictures that do **not** belong.

1

2

3

Stack Up

LOOK at the words and pictures. WRITE the names of the pictures in the correct columns.

shorts

sandals

earmuffs

swimsuit

scarf

mittens

Summer Clothes

_____

_____

_____

Winter Clothes

_____

_____

_____

Odd Word Out

CIRCLE the picture in each row that does **not** go with the others.

1.

five green yellow blue

2.

goat cow tiger pig

3.

bat rake hoe shovel

WRITE the names of the pictures that do **not** belong.

1

2

3

Stack Up

LOOK at the words and pictures. WRITE the names of the pictures in the correct columns.

daisy

pine

oak

rose

tulip

palm

willow

pansy

Flowers

_____

- - - - - - - - - - - - -

_____

- - - - - - - - - - - - -

_____

- - - - - - - - - - - - -

_____

Trees

_____

- - - - - - - - - - - - -

_____

- - - - - - - - - - - - -

_____

- - - - - - - - - - - - -

_____

Odd Word Out

CIRCLE the picture in each row that does **not** go with the others.

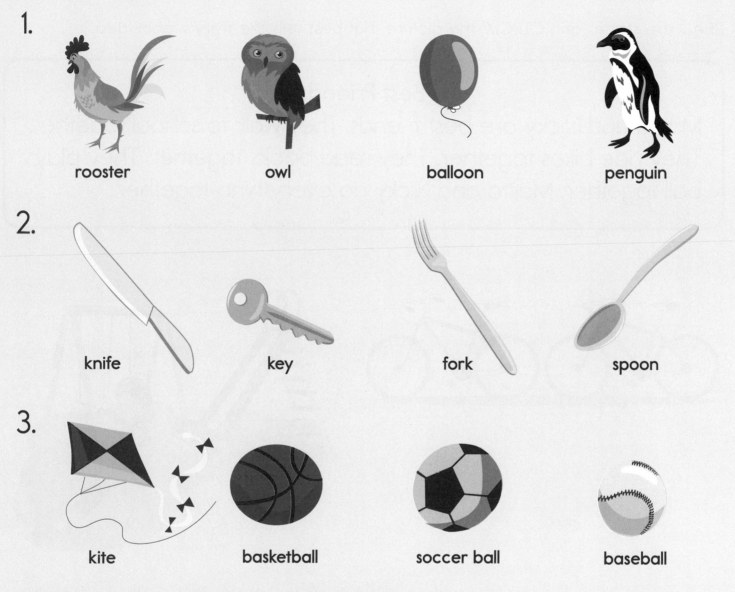

1. rooster   owl   balloon   penguin

2. knife   key   fork   spoon

3. kite   basketball   soccer ball   baseball

WRITE the names of the pictures that do **not** belong.

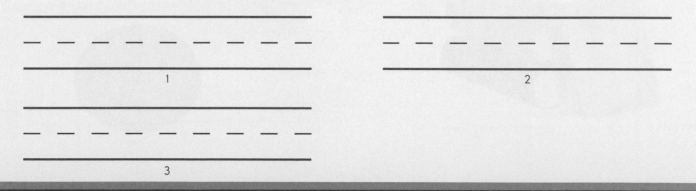

_____   _____

- - - - - - - - - - - - -   - - - - - - - - - - - - -

_____   _____
        1   2

_____

- - - - - - - - - - - - -

_____
        3

The Big Idea

It's All in the Picture

The **main idea** is the most important idea in a story. It's the big idea. It tells what the story is about.

READ the stories and CIRCLE the picture that best tells the story's main idea.

> ### Best Friends
> Marta and Nicky are best friends. They walk to school together. They ride bikes together. They read books together. They play ball together. Marta and Nicky do everything together.

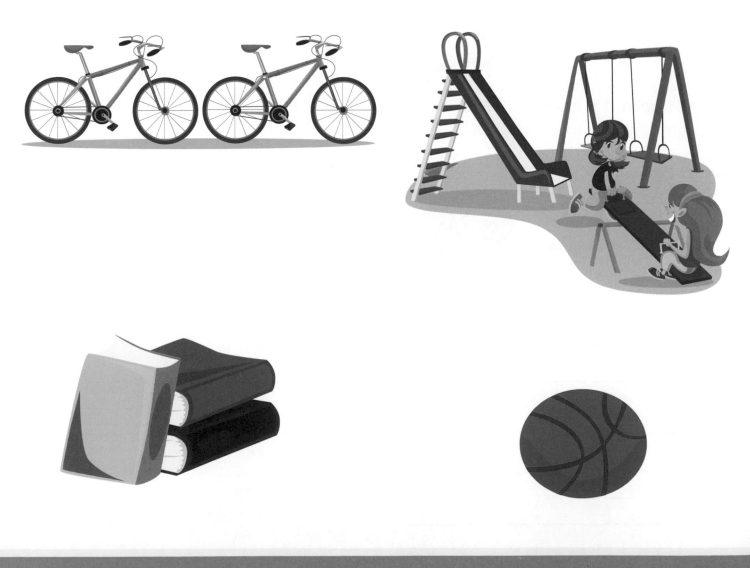

See and Hear Farm Animals

You can see and hear many animals on a farm. You can see horses. Horses neigh. You can see cows. Cows moo. You can see pigs. Pigs oink. What other animals can you see and hear on a farm?

The Big Idea

Name It

READ the stories. CHECK the box next to the best title for each story.

Trees are homes for many animals. Squirrels live in trees. They hide nuts in the trees.

Bees live in trees. They make hives in the trees.

Birds live in trees. They build nests in the trees.

Many animals live in trees.

☐ Bees and Hives

☐ Trees Are Homes

☐ Birds Make Nests

Rosa is a baker. One of the best cakes she ever made was for a man named Mr. Lee. He wanted a special cake for his wife's birthday party. Mrs. Lee loves cats. So Rosa made her a cake with cats on it.

Mrs. Lee thought the cake was the best cake she had ever seen. She did not want to cut it. Mr. Lee said that their guests were waiting to eat cake. Mrs. Lee almost cried when she had to cut the cake. But she loved the way it tasted.

☐ A Special Cake

☐ Cats Are Special

☐ A Birthday Party

The Big Idea

What's the Big Idea?

READ the stories. CHECK the sentence that tells the main idea.

Wishes

Have you ever wished for something? My little sister wishes for a new doll and new shoes. My big brother wishes for a computer and a car. I wish that I could fly and travel to the moon. What do you wish for?

☐ People make wishes.

☐ Wishing to fly is better than wishing for a new doll.

☐ You should be happy with what you have.

Buster

Buster likes to do a lot of things. He likes to fetch his rubber ball. He likes to chase butterflies and dig holes. He likes to have his tummy rubbed and his back scratched. But most of all, Buster loves to go for walks in the park.

☐ Buster can fetch a ball.

☐ Buster likes to do many things.

☐ Buster loves to go for walks.

Details, Details

Details tell about the main idea. They can tell who, what, where, when, and how. READ the story. CIRCLE the pictures that show details from the story.

Different but the Same

Lily and Nate are both different and the same. They are different because Lily is tall and Nate is short. Lily plays soccer and Nate plays baseball. Lily has a cat and Nate has a dog. Lily lives in an apartment and Nate lives in a house.

Lily and Nate are the same because Lily likes Nate just the way he is. And Nate likes Lily just the way she is. Lily and Nate say, "That's how friends are."

Who?

What?

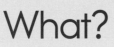

Where?

Details, Details

READ the story.

Careful Grace

It was a cold, snowy winter day. Papa and Grace drove a car to the park. They walked to the ice rink inside the park. Papa was going to teach Grace to ice skate.

Papa showed Grace how to put on her skates and how to walk in them. Grace held Papa's hand tightly as the two of them skated around the rink.

At last, Grace let go of Papa's hand. She began to glide on the ice. Papa waved at Grace. She waved back. She hoped that it was not time to stop.

READ each sentence. CIRCLE the picture that matches what happens in the story.

1. How do Papa and Grace get to the park?

2. What kind of day is it?

3. Where did Papa and Grace go?

Yes or No?

READ the story.

Mammals

A mammal is a certain kind of animal. Mammals have hair or fur. Mammals take good care of their babies. Mammals drink their mother's milk.

A tiger is a mammal that lives in the jungles of Asia. Its stripes help it hide in the tall grass.

A pig is a mammal that lives on a farm. It likes to eat corn and roll in the mud.

A bat is a mammal that lives in many places. It can fly.

A whale is a mammal that lives in the ocean. It must come up to breathe air.

Guess what? You are a mammal too!

READ each sentence. WRITE **true** if the sentence matches what you read in the story. WRITE **false** if it does not.

1. All mammals have feathers.

   _____

   - - - - -

   _____

2. Pigs like to eat corn.

   _____

   - - - - -

   _____

3. A whale does not need to breathe air.

   _____

   - - - - -

   _____

4. Humans are mammals.

   _____

   - - - - -

   _____

5. Tigers can hide in the tall grass.

   _____

   - - - - -

   _____

First, Next, Last

A story has a beginning, a middle, and an end. READ the story. What happens first? Next? Last? WRITE 1, 2, and 3 in the boxes to show the correct order.

Time to Garden

"Time to get up!" said Mom and Dad.

"Why?" asked Kate and Tim.

"We're going to plant a garden," said Mom and Dad.

Kate and Tim got up and got dressed. Then they ate breakfast.

Mom, Dad, Kate, and Tim drove to the garden shop. They bought flower seeds and some gardening tools.

When they got home, Dad dug up the dirt. Kate and Tim poked holes in the dirt. Kate and Tim put a few seeds in each hole. Then they covered the holes with dirt. Mom watered the seeds.

"Now we just have to wait," said Dad. "The plants will grow into pretty flowers," said Mom.

Kate and Tim smiled.

☐ Mom waters the garden.

☐ Kate and Tim plant the seeds.

☐ Dad digs up the dirt.

READ the story. What happens first? Next? Last? WRITE 1, 2, and 3 in the boxes to show the correct order.

Market Day

Today is market day. First Grandma and Juan stop by to see Mr. Sanchez the baker. The air is filled with delicious smells. Grandma buys two loaves of bread. When they leave, Mr. Sanchez hands Juan a cookie.

Their next stop is the fruit stand. They buy grapes, peaches, and plums. Grandma gets some flowers just before they leave.

At home, Grandma puts the flowers in a vase and Juan unpacks the food. Then he eats a ripe, juicy peach.

☐ Grandma and Juan stop at the baker's.

☐ Juan eats a peach.

☐ Grandma buys some flowers.

Order of Events

Picture Order

Sometimes stories have words like "first," "next," "after," and "last." These words give you clues about the order of events in the story.

LOOK at the pictures and READ the sentences. LOOK for the word clues. Then NUMBER the pictures from 1 to 4 to show the order in the stories.

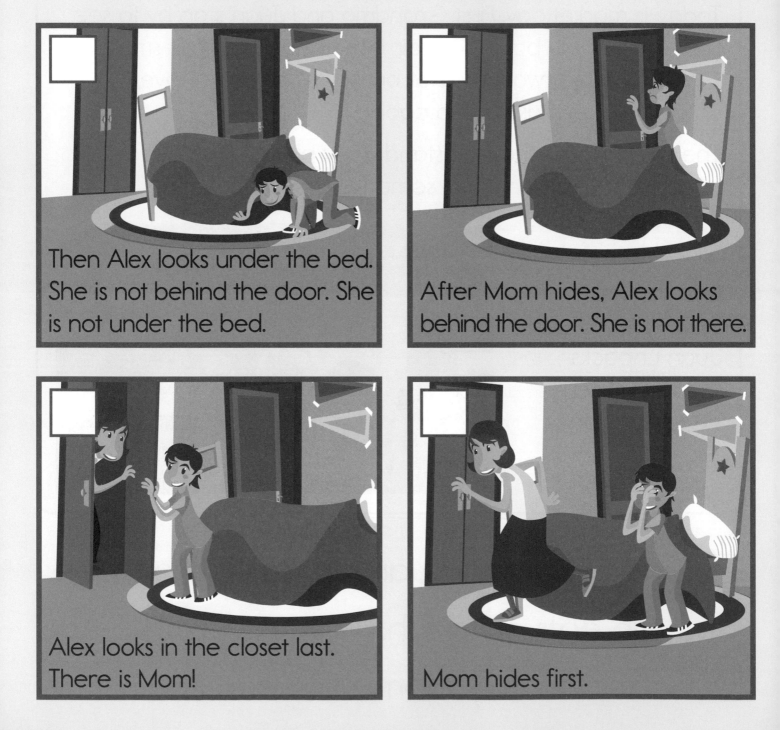

Then Alex looks under the bed. She is not behind the door. She is not under the bed.

After Mom hides, Alex looks behind the door. She is not there.

Alex looks in the closet last. There is Mom!

Mom hides first.

Finally, Mia puts the leaves into a big bag.

Then Mia rakes the leaves into a big pile.

First, Mia gets a rake.

Next, Mia begins to rake.

Story Order

READ the story.

Hello, Frog!

It's time for newborn frogs! A baby frog is called a tadpole. A tadpole has a large head. Its body is round. It has a long tail. It wiggles its long tail to help it swim. The tadpole grows fast. Its body gets bigger. It grows legs. Then it loses its tail. Now it is a frog.

Now NUMBER the pictures from 1 to 4 to show the order.

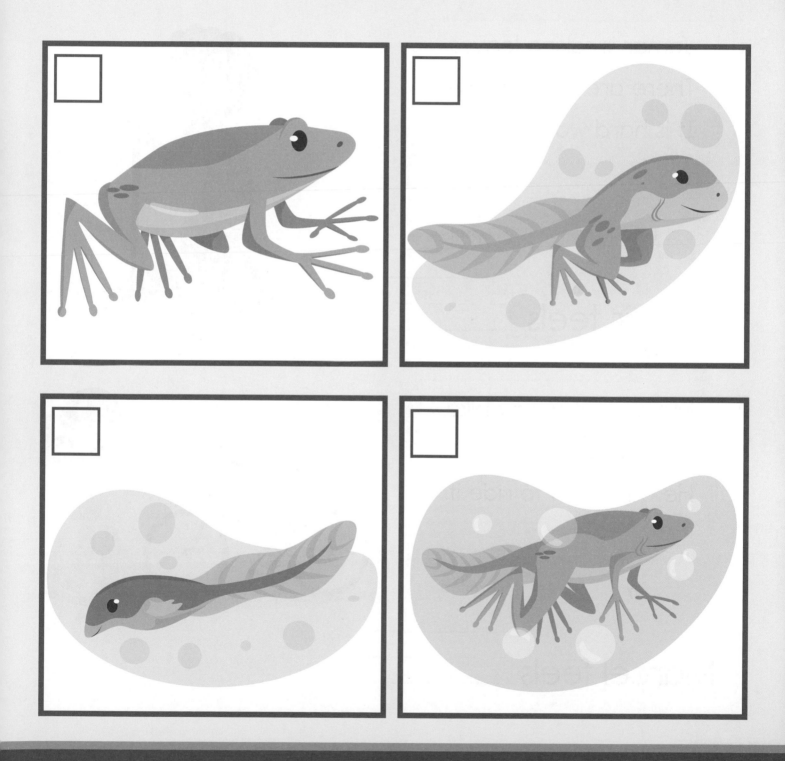

Reading between the Lines

Looking for Clues

Sometimes writers don't tell you everything in a story. You need to look for clues or "read between the lines" to think about what the writer means.

READ each story. LOOK at the picture for clues. FIND the word that best describes the person in the story to complete the sentence.

1. Jamar is raking leaves.
   There are a lot of leaves.
   It is hard work.

   tired   upset

   Jamar feels _____.

2. Marcel got a new bike.
   It is big and blue.
   He can't wait to ride it.

   silly   excited

   Marcel feels _____.

3.

Annie lost her ring.

She has looked everywhere for it.

Where could it be?

lucky   sad

Annie feels _____.

4.

Annie found her ring.
It was under her bed.

She puts the ring on her finger.

sleepy   happy

Annie feels _____.

Looking for Clues

READ each part of the story. THINK about what the writer is saying. Then CIRCLE the correct answer.

Beach Vacation

Jason and Jenna are going to camp at the beach. They help Mom and Dad get ready for the trip. They have to buy food. They have to pack the gear. They have to load the van.

1. Getting ready for a camping trip can be _____.

   a. a lot of work

   b. a waste of time

   c. too easy

The beach is a lot of fun. Jason and Jenna play in the sand. They search for shells. They dig for clams. They swim in the water. They help make the meals. Usually they just have cereal for breakfast and sandwiches for lunch. But for dinner, they fix something special.

Jason and Jenna like roasting hot dogs over the fire. Then it is time for bed.

2. What is it like to camp at the beach?
   a. boring
   b. busy
   c. scary

Looking for Clues

READ each part of the story. THINK about what the writer is saying. Then CIRCLE the correct answer.

Sparrow Finds a Friend

Sparrow had a problem. All the other birds were bigger than he was. Sparrow decided to look for other birds his size. He met Crow. But Crow was much bigger than he was.

He met Woodpecker. But Woodpecker was also much bigger than he was. Sparrow kept looking until he was too tired to fly any more. He rested.

A large plump bird waddled up to Sparrow.

1. What can you tell about Sparrow in this part of the story?
   a. He thinks a friend should be his size.
   b. He does not like Crow or Woodpecker.
   c. He wishes he were not a sparrow.

READ the next part of the story.

"Hello," she said, "I am Duck. You are a beautiful bird."

"No, I'm not. I am too small," said Sparrow.

"Your size makes you special," replied Duck. "Would you like to be my friend?"

"But we are not the same size," Sparrow said. "How can we be friends?"

Duck said, "We're both birds, aren't we? It doesn't matter that we are different."

The two birds flew off. Sparrow had found a new friend.

2. What can you tell about sparrow in this part of the story?
   a. He thinks Duck is a beautiful bird.
   b. He thinks it is better to be big.
   c. He wishes that Duck would go away.

Making Predictions

Pick the One

Sometimes you can tell or *predict* what a book is about by looking at the picture on the cover.

LOOK at the picture on each cover. CIRCLE the title that best shows what the story might be about.

1.

    a. *Time to Garden*

    b. *Learn to Skate*

    c. *Leaves Are Changing*

2.

a. Many Animals Live in Ponds

b. Ducks and Other Birds

c. Frog and Turtle Are Friends

3.

a. Water Play

b. Dog Wash

c. Time to Swim

Making Predictions

And Then . . .

READ the beginning of the story. Then PREDICT what will happen next. UNDERLINE the correct answer.

Sam's Vacation

Sam is going to stay with his uncle and aunt for the summer. They live on a farm.

Sam's mother grew up on a farm. She told Sam stories about how much fun she had on the farm. Sam was excited. But he worried about being away from home all summer. "There is so much to do," said Sam's mother. "You'll love it."

Sam was surprised when he first saw the farm. It looked so different from where he lived. He was used to seeing many cars and big buildings. Here he saw only a white house and a red barn.

The next morning, Sam woke up early. His uncle showed him how to milk a cow. After lunch, he learned how to feed the chickens and pigs.

After dinner, Sam got a phone call. It was his mother. She asked, "Did you enjoy your day?"

"I sure did," Sam said excitedly. "I can't wait for tomorrow."

What do you think Sam will do tomorrow?

a. Milk the cow and feed the chickens and pigs

b. Ask to go home

c. Stay inside all day

Detective Work

READ the story and LOOK for clues. PREDICT what will happen next. WRITE your prediction on the blank line.

Rosie's Problem

Rosie shook the coins out of her piggy bank. She had been saving for a long time. She counted the coins. She had saved ten dollars. But Rosie had a big problem. She did not know what to buy with her money. She asked her mom. She asked her dad. She even asked her little brother. No one had an answer. Mom said, "Why don't we go to the toy store?"

There were so many toys. Rosie looked at the toy cars. She looked at the dolls. She looked at the games. Rosie was sad. She did not know how to spend her money. "Let's just go home, Mom," Rosie sighed.

Someone was holding a box of puppies in front of the toy store. Rosie stopped and read the sign on the box. A big smile spread across her face. She knew exactly what to do.

How do you think Rosie most likely spent her money?

Rosie most likely spent her money on

_____

_ _

Fact or Opinion?

A **fact** is something that is true or can be proven. An **opinion** is something that is somebody's own idea.

READ the sentences. DECIDE if each sentence is a fact or an opinion. Then WRITE the sentences in the correct columns.

Orange juice tastes good.

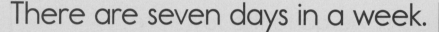

There are seven days in a week.

Earth has only one moon.

Blue is the prettiest color.

Dogs are the best pets ever.

Roses come in many colors.

Fact

_____

- -

_____

_____

- -

_____

_____

- -

_____

Opinion

_____

- -

_____

_____

- -

_____

_____

- -

_____

Fact or Opinion?

READ the story. Then READ the sentences on the next page. WRITE **F** if the sentence is a fact. WRITE **O** if the sentence is somebody's opinion.

A Funny Bird

Penguins are interesting birds. Penguins cannot fly. But they can swim fast. They are shaped like a bullet. This helps them swim. They use their wings to move themselves through the water.

Penguins cannot breathe underwater. But they can hold their breath for a long time.

The only time penguins are in the air is when they leap out of the water to get on land. They also jump high into the air to get a gulp of air before diving back down for fish. They look funny when they do this. Penguins are interesting animals.

1. Penguins are interesting birds. _____

2. Penguins cannot fly. _____

3. They use their wings to move themselves through the water. _____

4. Penguins cannot breathe underwater. _____

5. They look funny when they do this. _____

Details, Details

READ the story. Then ANSWER the questions on the next page.

Yoli woke up early. "What day is it?" asked Yoli.

"Saturday," said Mom.

"Yippee!" yelled Yoli. "It's time to go shopping."

Yoli went to a yard sale first. "Yoo-hoo! Do you have any yarn for sale?" she asked.

"Yes, I have yarn for sale," said a man.

"Yippie!" yelled Yoli. She put the yarn inside her bag.

Yoli went to the toy store next. "Yoo-hoo! Do you have any yo-yos for sale?" she asked.

"Yes, I have yo-yos for sale," said the clerk.

"Yippie!" yelled Yoli. She put a yo-yo inside her bag.

Then Yoli went to the grocery store. "Yoo-hoo! Do you have any yams for sale?" she asked.

"Yes, I have yams for sale," said the grocer.

"Yippie!" yelled Yoli. She put a yam inside her bag.

Yoli went to the bakery last. "Yoo-hoo! Do you have any yellow cupcakes for sale?" she asked.

"Yes, I have yellow cupcakes for sale," said the baker.

"Yippie!" yelled Yoli. She put a yellow cupcake inside her bag. Yoli said, "I am hungry." So she went home to lunch.

CIRCLE the best name for this story. Think about the main idea of the story.

Yoli Goes Shopping   The Yard Sale   Yarn and Yams

CIRCLE the correct details from the story.

1. What does Yoli buy at the toy store?
   a. a kite b. a ball c. a yo-yo

2. Who sells yams?
   a. the baker b. the grocer c. the toy clerk

3. What color is the cupcake?
   a. yellow b. pink c. green

4. When does Yoli go shopping?
   a. in the morning b. at noon c. at night

Answers

Page 2
1. bike
2. bed
3. fish
4. goat
5. dog
6. desk
7. bus
8. fork
9. doll
10. gum

Page 3

Page 4
1. quick, quit
2. jeans, jam
3. kite, kick
4. hand
5. keep

Page 5
1. hand
2. king
3. queen
4. jar
5. kite
6. quilt
7. hat
8. jug

Page 6
l: leaf, log
m: mat, mop
n: nose, net
p: pan, pig

Page 7

Page 8
1. tent
2. ring
3. tooth
4. rooster
5. tomato
6. seal
7. six
8. red
9. tub
10. saw

Page 9

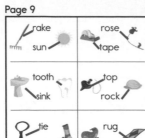

Page 10
v: van, vase
w: wig, web
y: yellow, yo-yo
z: zipper, zebra

Page 11

1. van
2. vest
3. wing
4. x-ray
5. yarn
6. zero

Page 12
1. kid, cage
2. cent, sip
3. get, give
4. jump, gem

Page 13

Page 14
1. red
2. sub
3. mop
4. drum
5. fan
6. hand
7. crib
8. ram
9. top
10. moon

Page 15
1. gum, clam
2. moon
3. food, sad
4. jump, top
5. rub

Page 16

1. goat
2. bell
3. flag
4. dress
5. fork

Page 17

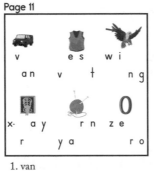

Page 18
1. mitten
2. seven
3. pillow
4. hammer
5. zipper
6. robot
7. lemon
8. kitten
9. ladder
10. puppy

Page 19
1. metal
2. jacket
3. hammer
4. jelly
5. wagon

Page 20
1. thumb
2. shell
3. chair
4. shoe
5. shirt
6. ship
7. shark
8. cherry
9. thimble
10. cheese

Page 21
1. splash
2. moth
3. beach
4. brush
5. bench

Page 22

Page 23

Page 24
1. bed
2. nest
3. sled
4. net
5. web
6. pen

Page 25
1. nest
2. egg
3. ten
4. web
5. bed

Page 26

pig
bib
fish
pin
quilt

Answers

Page 27
1. dish, wish
2. pit
3. bib
4. big, wig
5. mix

Page 28

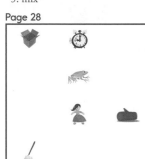

Page 29

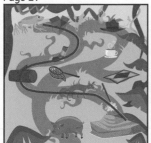

Page 30
1. plug
2. rug
3. bus
4. sun
5. mud
6. tub

Page 31
1. rug
2. cup
3. sub
4. gum
5. truck

Page 32

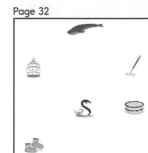

Page 33

Page 34
1. tree
2. knee
3. queen
4. bee
5. green
6. sheep

Page 35
1. bee
2. green
3. wheel
4. three
5. heel

Page 36

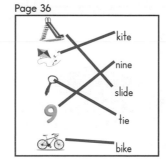

Page 37
1. bite
2. hive
3. tie
4. wipe, ripe
5. fine, dine

Page 38

Page 39

Page 40
1. blue
2. flute
3. tube
4. mule
5. cube
6. glue

Page 41
1. mule
2. cube
3. flute
4. glue
5. blue

Page 42

Page 43
1. fry
2. July
3. city
4. fairy
5. cherry

Page 44
1. cupcake
2. starfish
3. doorbell
4. raincoat
5. ladybug

Page 45
1. doghouse
2. snowman
3. catfish
4. football
5. rainbow

Page 46
1. sailboat
2. bedroom
3. pancake
4. sandbox
5. seashell
6. peanut
7. spaceship

Page 47
1. backyard = back + yard
2. baseball = base + ball
3. butterfly = butter + fly
4. backpack = back + pack
5. goldfish = gold + fish

Page 48
1. I'll → I will
2. we're → we are
3. it's → it is
4. weren't → were not
5. I'm → I am

Page 49

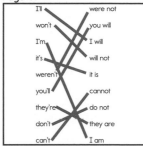

Page 50
1. din|ner, din, ner
2. kit|ten, kit, ten
3. mit|ten, mit, ten
4. hap|pen, hap, pen
5. pup|pet, pup, pet
6. zip|per, zip, per
7. muf|fin, muf, fin
8. but|ton, but, ton

Page 51
1. ple
2. mer
3. ten
4. za
5. py
6. low

Page 52
1. nap|kin, nap, kin
2. bas|ket, bas, ket
3. doc|tor, doc, tor
4. pic|nic, pic, nic
5. mon|key, mon, key
6. win|ter, win, ter
7. sis|ter, sis, ter
8. pen|cil, pen, cil

Page 53
1. wal
2. tur
3. tur
4. roos
5. mon
6. pen

Page 54
1. cats
2. kite
3. drum
4. roses
5. cakes
6. frogs

Answers

Page 55
1. gifts
2. maps
3. kites
4. books
5. cups
6. dogs
7. birds
8. cakes

Page 56
1. es
2. es
3. es
4. s
5. s
6. s
7. es
8. es

Page 57
1. leaves
2. loaves
3. knife
4. calves
5. wolves
6. elf

Page 58
1. teeth
2. geese
3. children
4. oxen
5. women
6. mice

Page 59
1. feet
2. teeth
3. children
4. geese
5. men
6. ox
7. fireman
8. person
9. mouse
10. woman

Page 60
1. round
2. just
3. four
4. fly
5. old
6. sleep

Page 61
1. fly
2. four
3. old
4. sleep
5. round
6. just

Page 62

1. very old
2. went to sleep
3. just think
4. four of them
5. is round
6. can fly

Page 63
1. fly
2. four
3. round
4. just
5. old

Page 64
1. sing
2. green
3. open
4. over
5. stop
6. give

Page 65
1. green
2. open
3. over
4. stop
5. give

Page 66

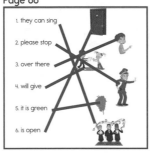

1. they can sing
2. please stop
3. over there
4. will give
5. it is green
6. is open

Page 67
1. stop
2. give
3. open
4. sing
5. green

Page 68
Fruits: lemon, apple, orange, grapes
Vegetables: corn, carrot, broccoli, lettuce

Page 69
1. olive
2. dog
3. yarn

Page 70
Summer clothes: shorts, sandals, swimsuit
Winter clothes: earmuffs, scarf, mittens

Page 71
1. five
2. tiger
3. bat

Page 72
Flowers: daisy, rose, tulip, pansy
Trees: pine, oak, palm, willow

Page 73
1. balloon
2. key
3. kite

Page 74

Page 75

Page 76
Trees Are Homes

Page 77
A Special Cake

Page 78
People make wishes.

Page 79
Buster likes to do many things.

Page 81

Page 83

Page 85
1. false
2. true
3. false
4. true
5. true

Page 86
3 Mom waters the garden.
2 Kate and Tim plant the seeds.
1 Dad digs up the dirt.

Page 87
1 Grandma and Juan stop at the baker's.
3 Juan eats a peach.
2 Grandma buys some flowers.

Page 88

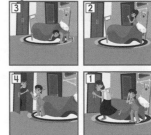

Page 89

Page 91

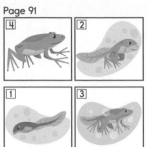

Pages 92–93
1. tired
2. excited
3. sad
4. happy

Pages 94–95
1. a
2. b

Pages 96–97
1. a
2. b

Pages 98–99
1. b
2. a
3. b

Page 100
a. Milk the cow and feed the
   chickens and pigs

Page 101
Suggestion: a puppy

Page 103
Fact
There are seven days in a week.
Earth has only one moon.
Roses come in many colors.
Opinion
Orange juice tastes good.
Blue is the prettiest color.
Dogs are the best pets ever.

Page 105
1. Opinion
2. Fact
3. Fact
4. Fact
5. Opinion

Page 107
Main idea: Yoli Goes Shopping
1. c
2. b
3. a
4. a

1st Grade
Spelling Games & Activities

Spell Short A

Slide Words

Let's make words that have a short **a** sound. DRAW a line between each picture and the ending that matches. Then WRITE the first letter of each word.

ram
1

at
2

ap
3

an
4

Fast Words

Can you SAY this sentence three times fast? Try it!

Pat's fat cat sat.

Now WRITE your own sentence. Use these words or other short **a** words. You can use words more than once. Then SAY the sentence three times fast!

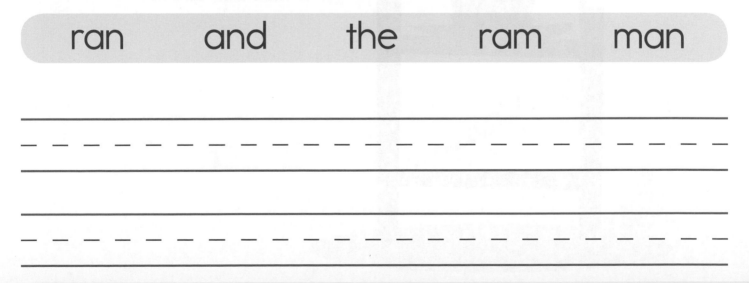

| ran | and | the | ram | man |

Spell Short A

Letter Ladder

Let's make more words with the short **a** sound. IDENTIFY the pictures on the ladder. Then WRITE the words next to the pictures.

HINT: You can change just one letter to make each new word.

r__a__m
1

__a__
2

__a__
3

__a__
4

Around We Go!

CIRCLE the things that have a short **a** sound.

WRITE the words with short **a** on the lines.

_____   _____   _____

_____   _____   _____

Make It Rhyme

CIRCLE the picture that makes a rhyme. WRITE the rhyming word in the space.

The ram eats a _____.

1

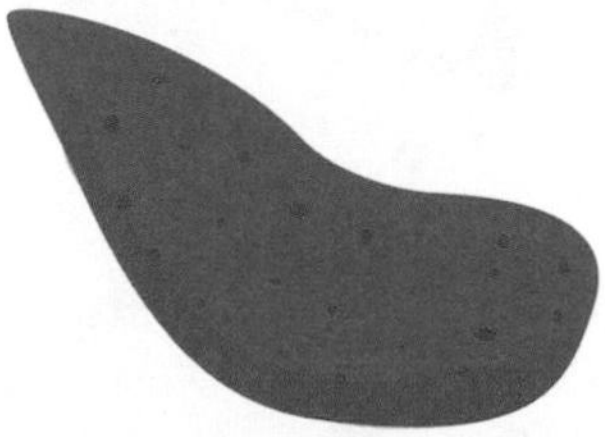

The fan cools the _____.

2

The hat is on the _____.

3

Space Walk Words

Make three-letter words with short **a**. START on a blue planet. GO to the green planet. Then GO to another blue planet.

Example:

bat

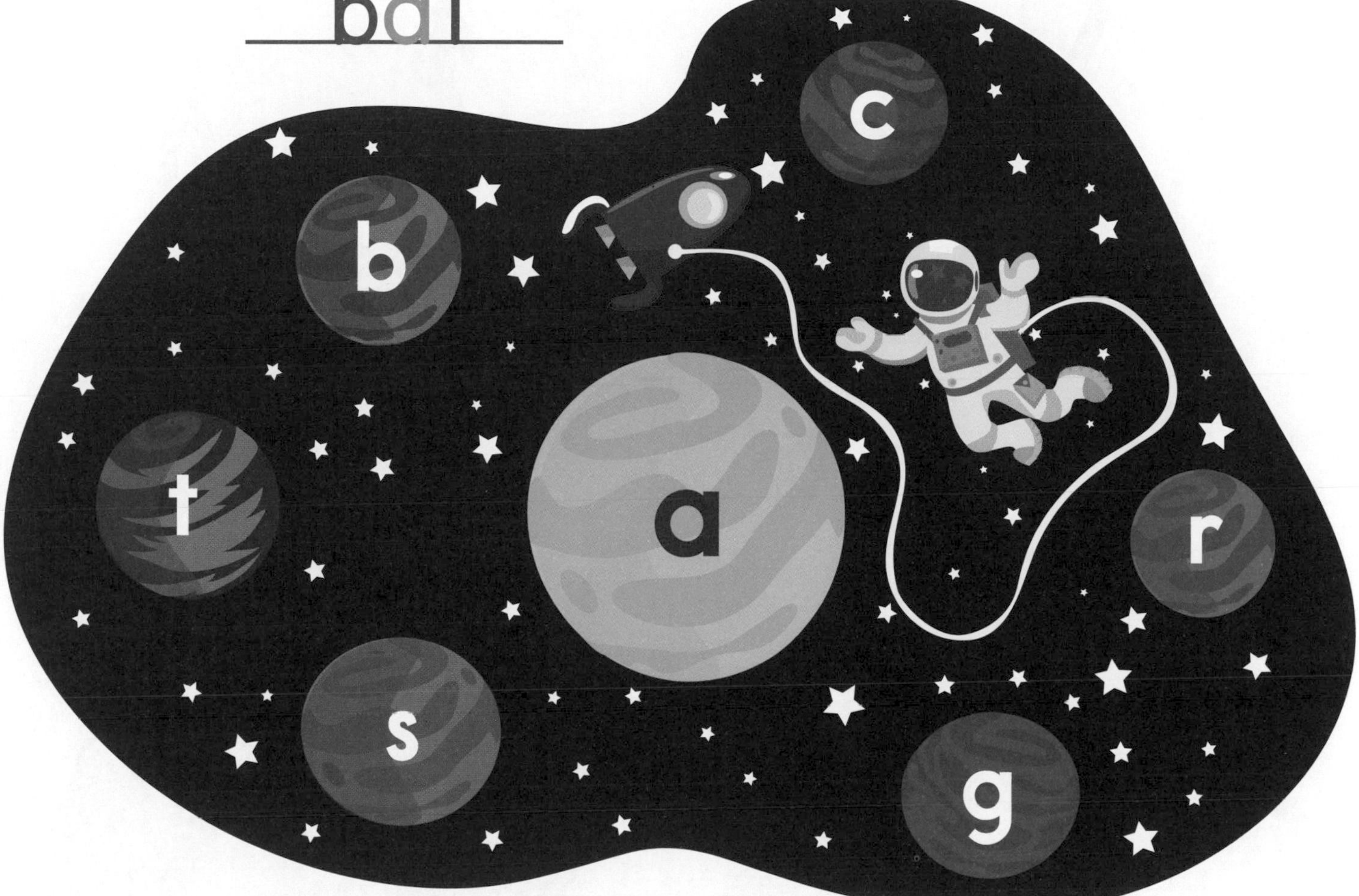

WRITE the words here.

_____

_ _ _ _ _ _ _

_____

_____

_ _ _ _ _ _ _

_____

Spell Short E

Slide Words

Let's make words that have a short **e** sound. DRAW a line between each picture and the ending that matches. Then WRITE the first letter of each word.

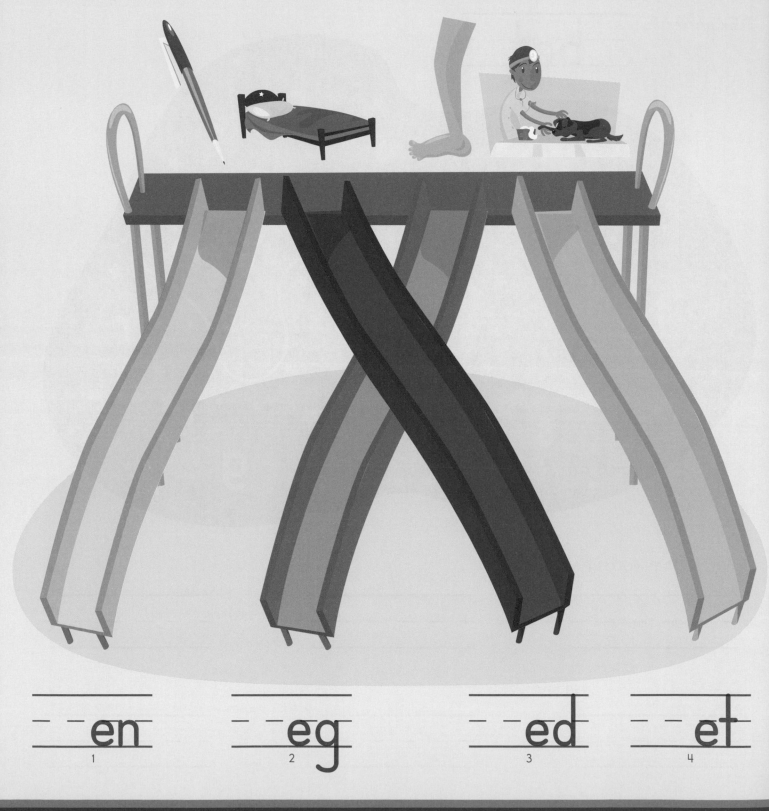

en
1

eg
2

ed
3

et
4

Letter Liftoff

FILL IN the first letter of each short **e** word.

_ en
1

_ ed
2

10
_ en
3

_ en
4

_ et
5

Around We Go!

CIRCLE the things that have a short **e** sound.

WRITE the words with short **e** on the lines.

_____   _____   _____

Fast Words

Can you SAY this sentence three times fast? Try it!

Ten men fed ten hens.

Now WRITE your own sentence. Use these words or other short **e** words. Then SAY the sentence three times fast!

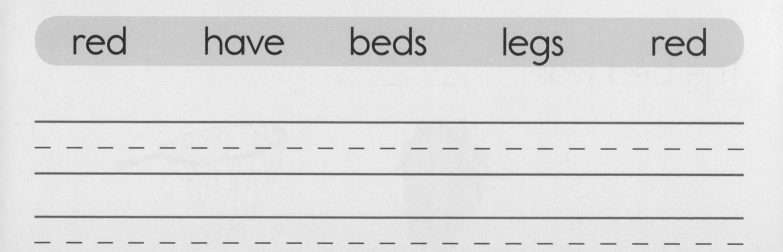

red   have   beds   legs   red

Make It Rhyme

CIRCLE the picture that makes a rhyme. WRITE the rhyming word in the space.

The wet pet saw the _____.
1

The hen has a _____.
2

The bed was _____.
3

Space Walk Words

Make three-letter words with short **e**. START on a blue planet. GO to the green planet. Then GO to another blue planet.

WRITE the words here.

_____   _____   _____

- - - - - - - - - - -   - - - - - - - - - - -   - - - - - - - - - - -

_____   _____   _____

- - - - - - - - - - -   - - - - - - - - - - -   - - - - - - - - - - -

Spell Numbers

How Many at the Market?

Spell Numbers 3

How many things can we buy at the market? WRITE a number word under each food.

one two three four five six seven eight

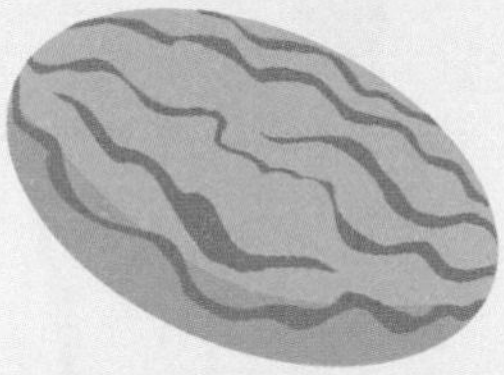

one

1

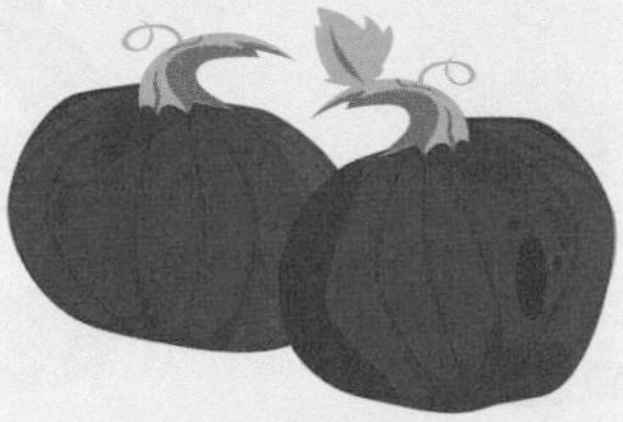

2

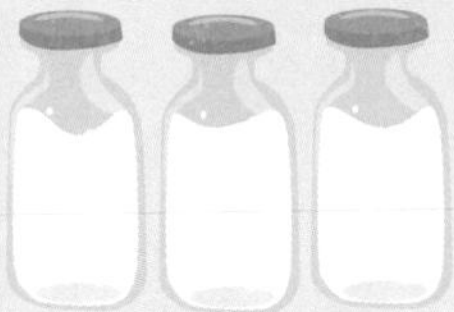

3

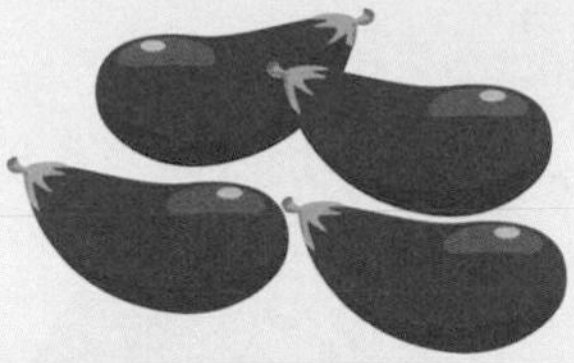

4

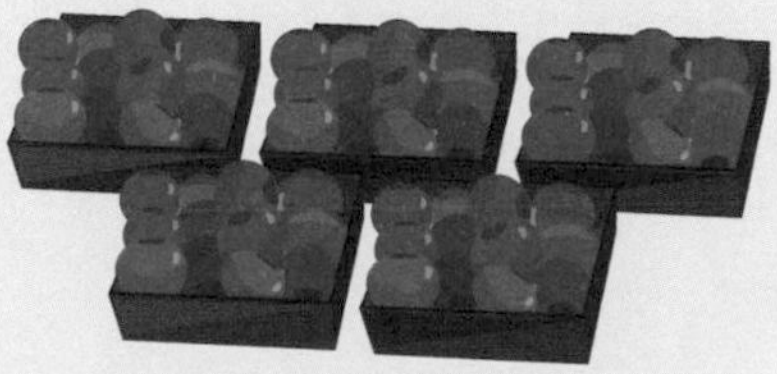

5

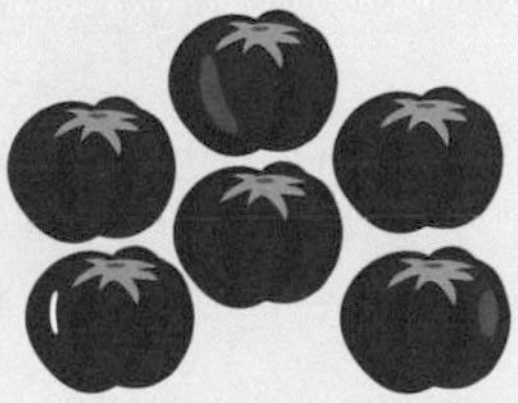

6

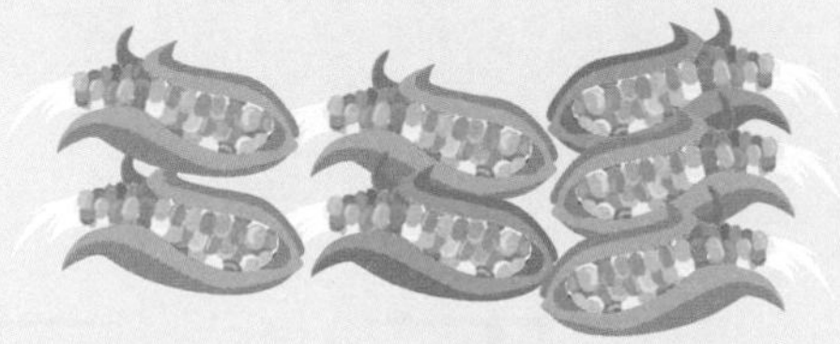

7

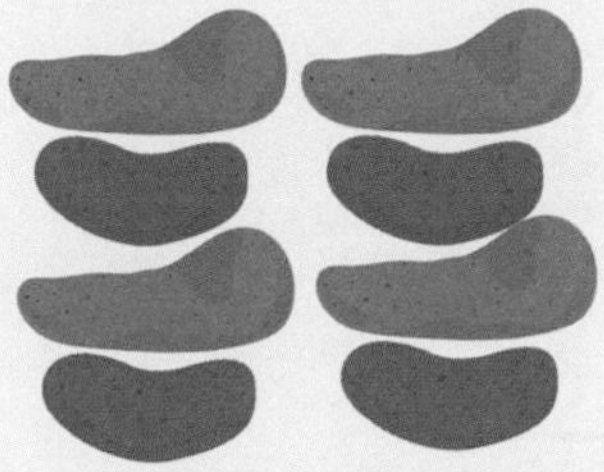

8

Spell Short I

Slide Words

Let's make words that have a short **i** sound. DRAW a line between each picture and the ending that matches. Then WRITE the first letter of each word.

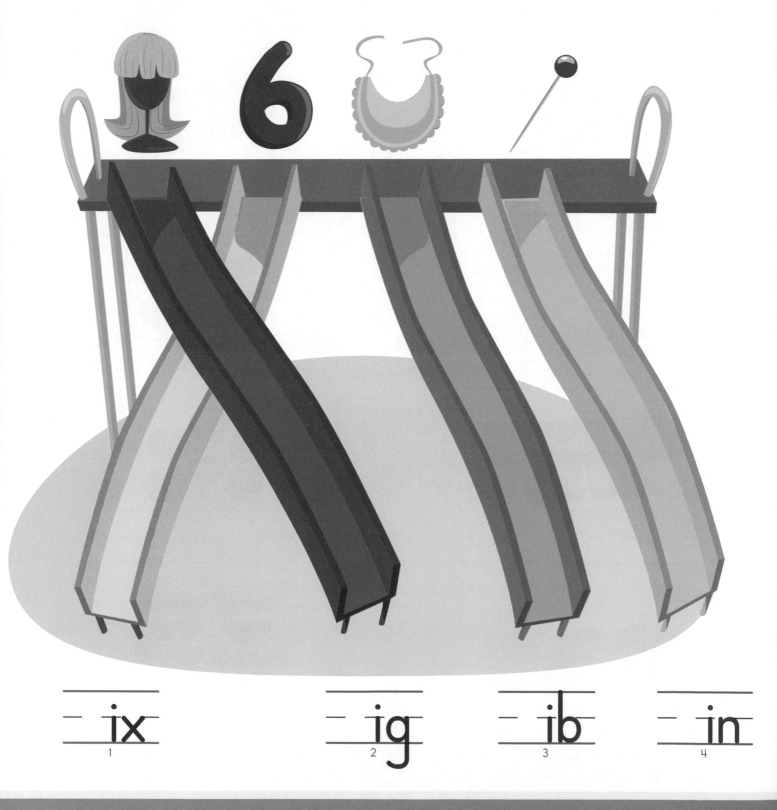

___ix
1

___ig
2

___ib
3

___in
4

Around We Go!

CIRCLE the things that have a short **i** sound.

WRITE the words with short **i** on the lines.

_____   _____   _____

_ _ _ _ _ _   _ _ _ _ _ _   _ _ _ _ _ _

_____   _____   _____

Fast Words

Can you SAY this sentence three times fast? Try it!

Six big pigs sit.

Now WRITE your own sentence. Use these words or other short **i** words. Then SAY the sentence three times fast!

pigs	kids	big	dig

_____

_____

_____

Letter Ladder

Let's make more words with the short **i** sound. IDENTIFY the pictures on the ladder.
Then WRITE the words next to the pictures.

HINT: You can change just one letter to make each new word.

1

2

3

4

Spell Short I

Make It Rhyme

CIRCLE the picture that makes a rhyme. WRITE the rhyming word in the space.

The pig lost her _____ .

1

My pin fell in the _____ .

2

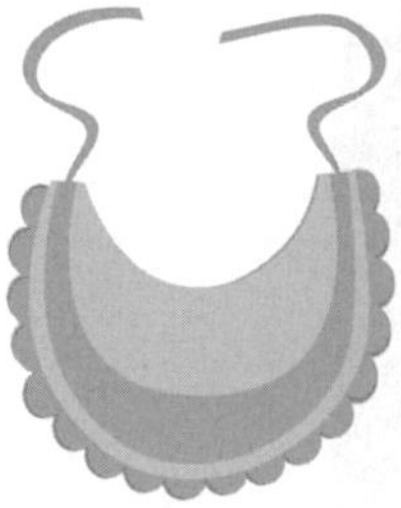

"Help me dig," said the _____ .

3

Space Walk Words

Make three-letter words with short **i**. START on a blue planet. GO to the orange planet. Then GO to another blue planet.

WRITE the words here.

_____   _____   _____

_____   _____   _____

Spell Short O

Slide Words

Let's make words that have a short **o** sound. DRAW a line between each picture and the ending that matches. Then WRITE the first letter of each word.

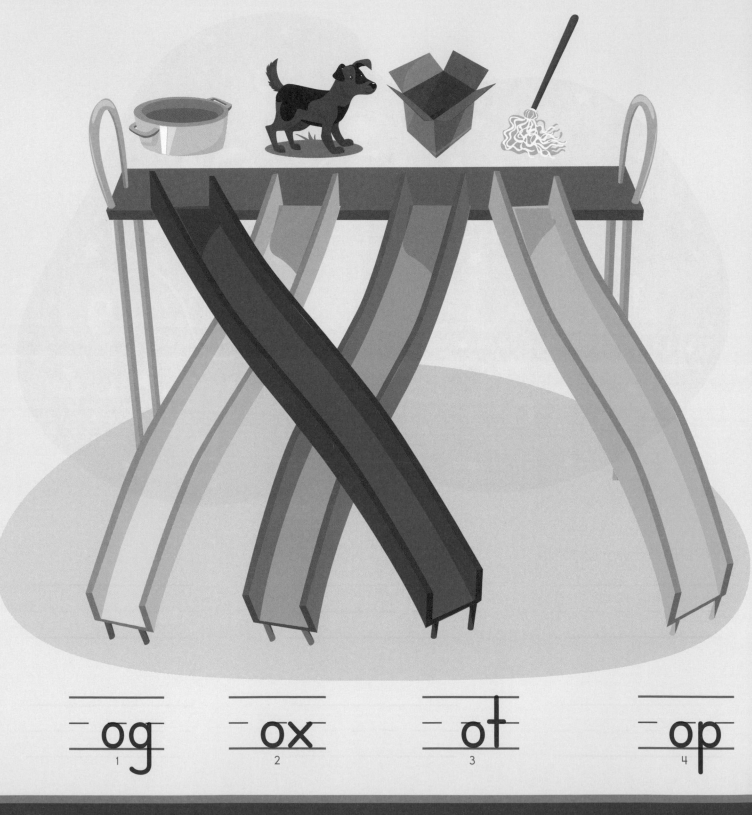

og
1

ox
2

ot
3

op
4

Letter Ladder

Let's make more words with the short **o** sound. IDENTIFY the pictures on the ladder. Then WRITE the words next to the pictures.

HINT: You can change just one letter to make each new word.

O
1

O
2

O
3

O
4

Make It Rhyme

CIRCLE the picture that makes a rhyme. WRITE the rhyming word in the space.

The dog jumps on a _____ .

The box is on top of the _____ .

Can you hop over the _____ ?

Fast Words

Can you SAY this sentence three times fast? Try it!

Hot pot tops pop.

Now WRITE your own sentence. Use these words or other short **o** words. Then SAY the sentence three times fast!

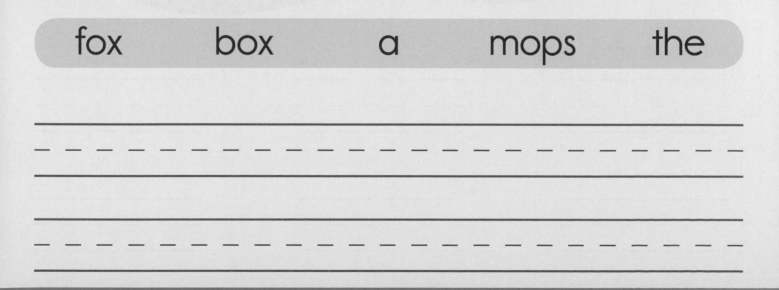

fox   box   a   mops   the

_____

_____

_____

Spell Short O

Space Walk Words

Make three-letter words with short **o**. START on a blue planet. GO to the green planet. Then GO to another blue planet.

WRITE the words here.

_____   _____   _____

- - - - - - -   - - - - - - -   - - - - - - -

_____   _____   _____

_____   _____   _____

- - - - - - -   - - - - - - -   - - - - - - -

_____   _____   _____

Riddle Me This!

UNSCRAMBLE the words to read the riddle.

Q: What **ogd** pops out of a **tpo**

_____   _____
- - - - - - - -   - - - - - - - -
_____   _____

that is **oht?**

_____
- - - - - - - -
_____

A: A hot dog!

Slide Words

Let's make words that have a short **u** sound. DRAW a line between each picture and the ending that matches. Then WRITE the first letter of each word.

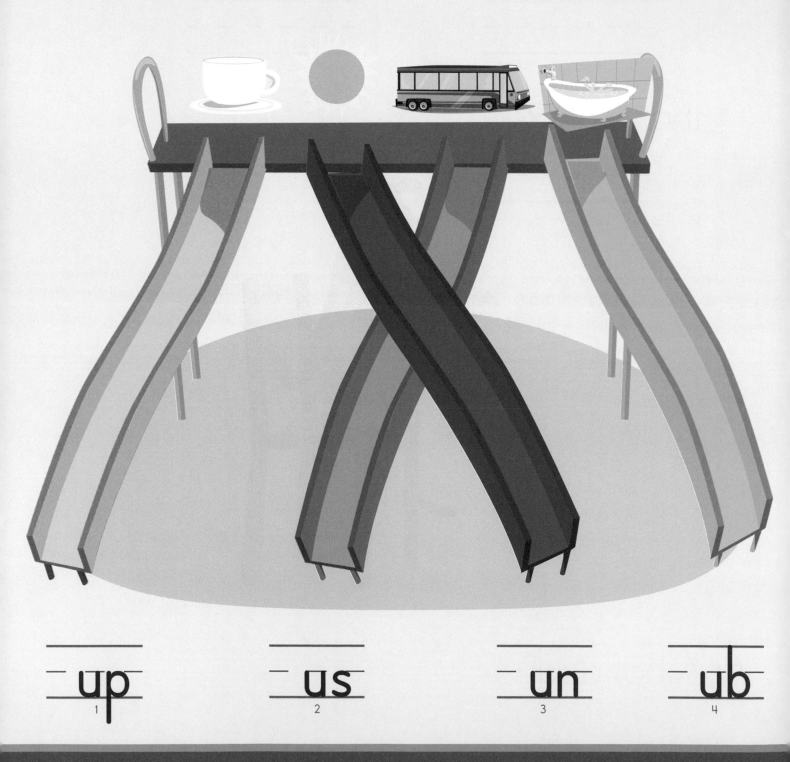

up
1

us
2

un
3

ub
4

Make It Rhyme

CIRCLE the picture that makes a rhyme. WRITE the rhyming word in the space.

The cub jumped in the _____ .
1

The pup found a _____ .
2

The bug hid under the _____ .
3

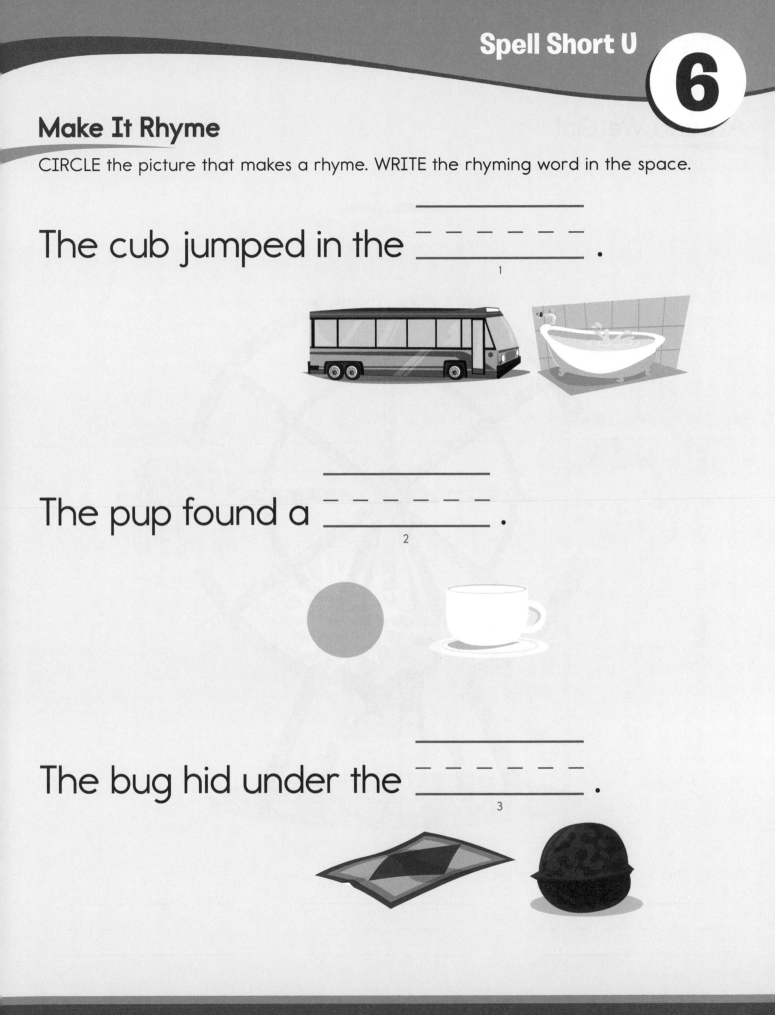

Spell Short U

Around We Go!

CIRCLE the things that have a short **u** sound.

WRITE the words with short **u** on the lines.

_____   _____   _____

_ _ _ _ _ _   _ _ _ _ _ _   _ _ _ _ _ _

Riddle Me This!

UNSCRAMBLE the words in the riddle.

Q: Why did the ubg drive

_____

– – – – – –

_____

his usb into the btu?

_____   _____

– – – – – –   – – – – – –

_____   _____

A: To get wheel-y wet!

Space Walk Words

Make three-letter words with short **u**. START on a blue planet. GO to the green planet. Then GO to another blue planet.

WRITE the words here.

_____   _____   _____
- - - - - - - - -   - - - - - - - - -   - - - - - - - - -

_____   _____   _____
- - - - - - - - -   - - - - - - - - -   - - - - - - - - -

_____   _____   _____
- - - - - - - - -   - - - - - - - - -   - - - - - - - - -

Criss Cross

READ the clues. FILL IN the short **u** words in the boxes.

| nut | bug | tub | sun | mud | hut | bus | but | gum |

Across

1. A small house is a _____.

3. It takes kids to school.

5. A little insect

7. A _____ has a hard shell.

8. This makes pigs dirty.

Down

2. Where you take a bath

4. The _____ shines in the sky.

5. I ran fast _____ did not win the race.

6. You can chew this.

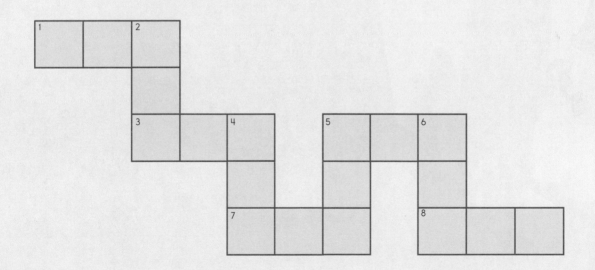

Living Colors

Spell Color Words

7

LOOK at all the colors in the market. WRITE a color word under each food.

red blue yellow orange green purple brown white

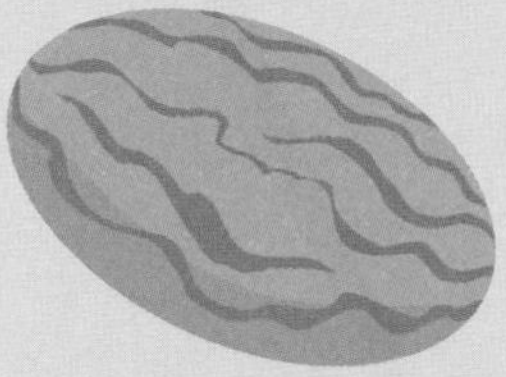

1

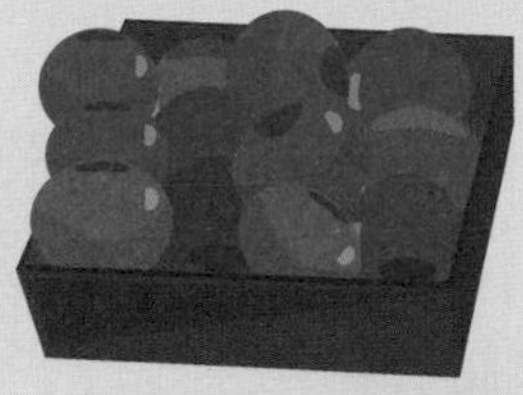

2

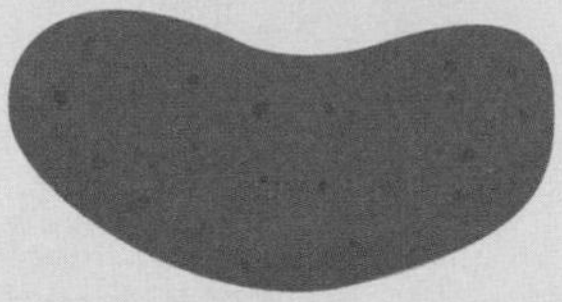

3

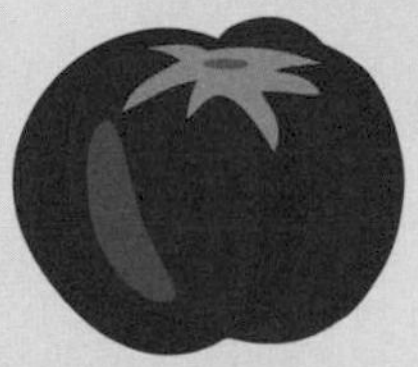

4

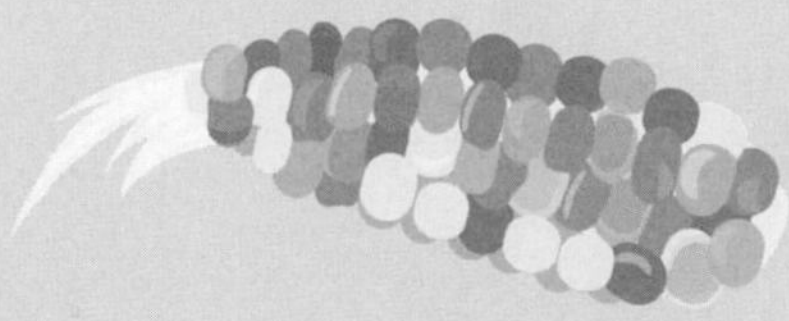

5

6

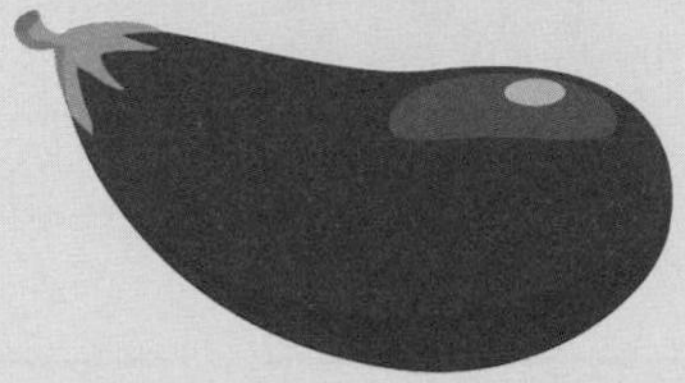

7

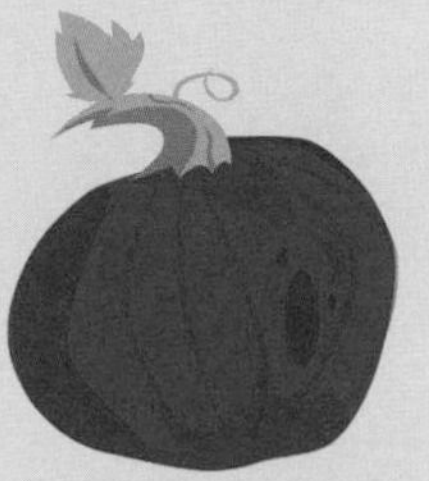

8

Slide Words

Let's make words that have a long **a** sound. DRAW a line between each picture and the ending that matches. Then WRITE the first letter of each word.

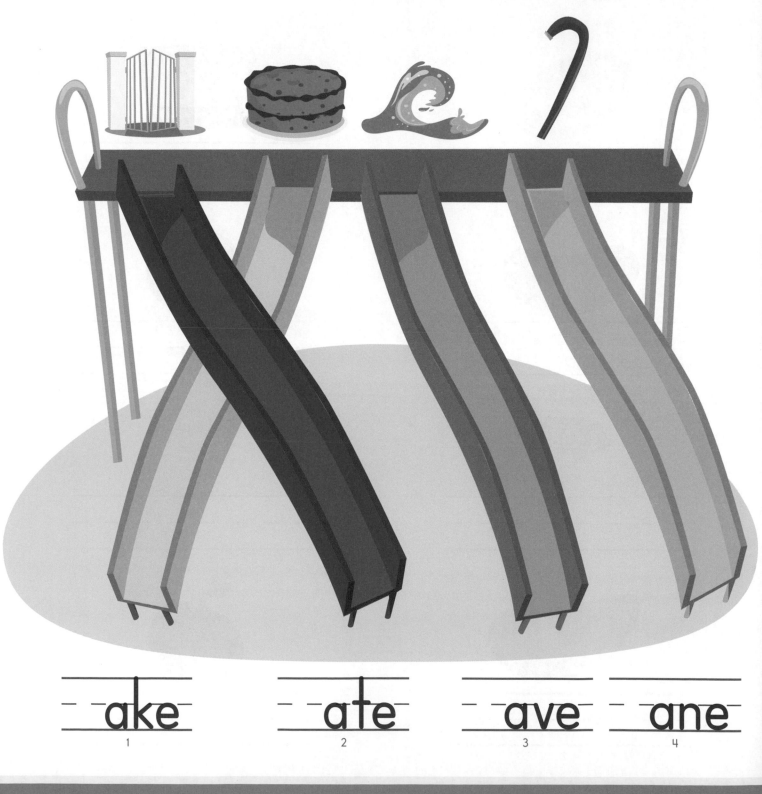

ake
1

ate
2

ave
3

ane
4

Letter Ladder

Let's make more words with the long **a** sound. IDENTIFY the pictures on the ladder. Then WRITE the words next to the pictures.

HINT: You can change just one letter to make each new word.

a e
1

a e
2

a e
3

a e
4

Spell Long A

Around We Go!

CIRCLE the things that have a long **a** sound.

WRITE the words with long **a** on the lines.

_____   _____   _____
_ _ _ _ _ _ _   _ _ _ _ _ _ _   _ _ _ _ _ _ _
_____   _____   _____

Fast Words

Can you SAY this sentence three times fast? Try it!

An ape in a cape came with a cake.

Now WRITE your own sentence. Use these words or other long **a** words. Then SAY the sentence three times fast!

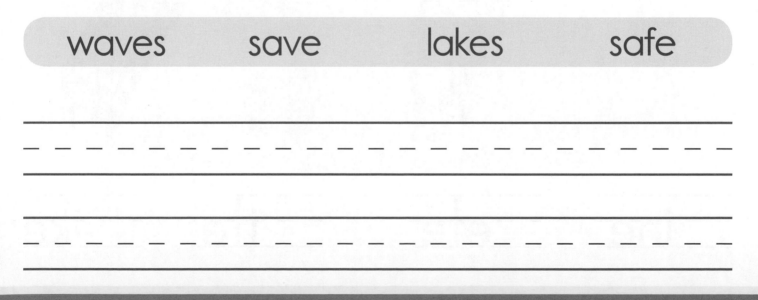

waves   save   lakes   safe

Spell Long E and I

Slide Words

Let's make words that have a long **e** or long **i** sound. DRAW a line between each picture and the ending that matches. Then WRITE the first letter of each word.

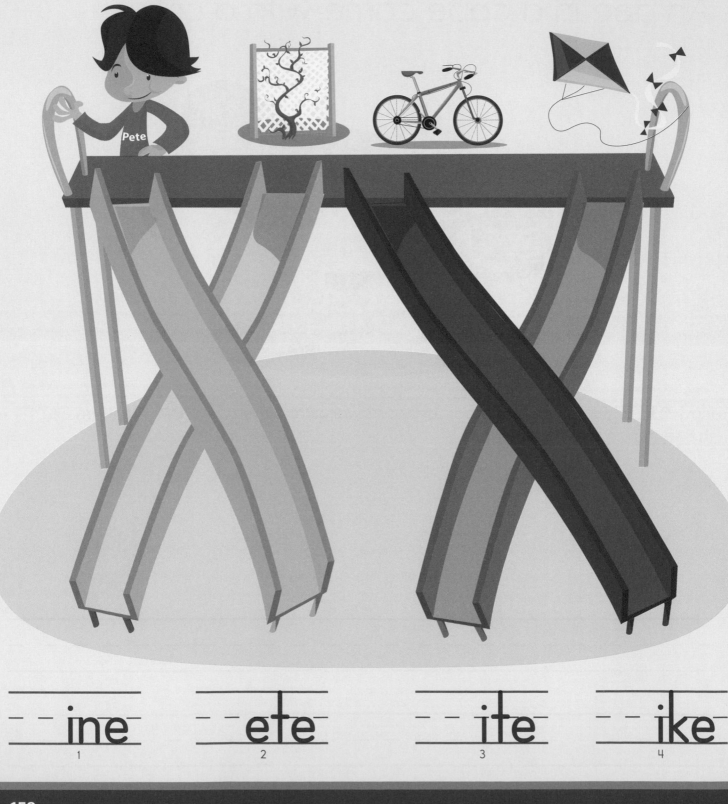

ine
1

ete
2

ite
3

ike
4

Letter Liftoff

FILL IN the vowel for each long **e** or long **i** word.

P _ te
1

p _ pe
2

b _ ke
3

k _ te
4

n _ ne
5

Spell Long E and I

Fast Words

Can you SAY this sentence three times fast? Try it!

Five fine vines are mine.

Now WRITE your own sentence. Use these words or other long **i** words. Then SAY the sentence three times fast!

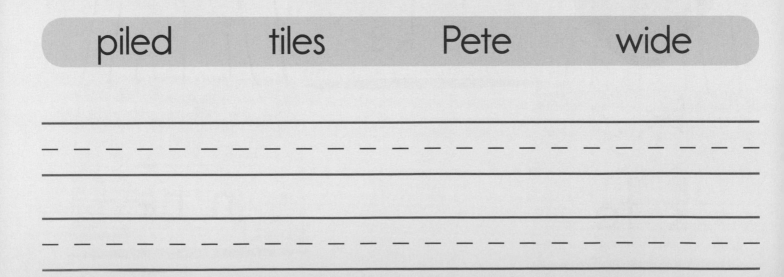

piled   tiles   Pete   wide

_____

- -

_____

- -

_____

Criss Cross

READ the clues. FILL IN the long **e** and **i** words in the boxes.

bike	kite	pipe	time	Pete	dime	bite	nine

Across

2. Ten cents

3. Water goes through this to get
   to your bathtub

4. It comes before ten.

5. A clock tells you the _____.

6. A short word for *bicycle*

Down

1. This flies up in the sky.

3. A nickname for Peter

6. When you eat, you take a big _____.

Spell Long O and U

Slide Words

Let's make words that have a long **o** sound. DRAW a line between each picture and the ending that matches. Then WRITE the first letter of each word.

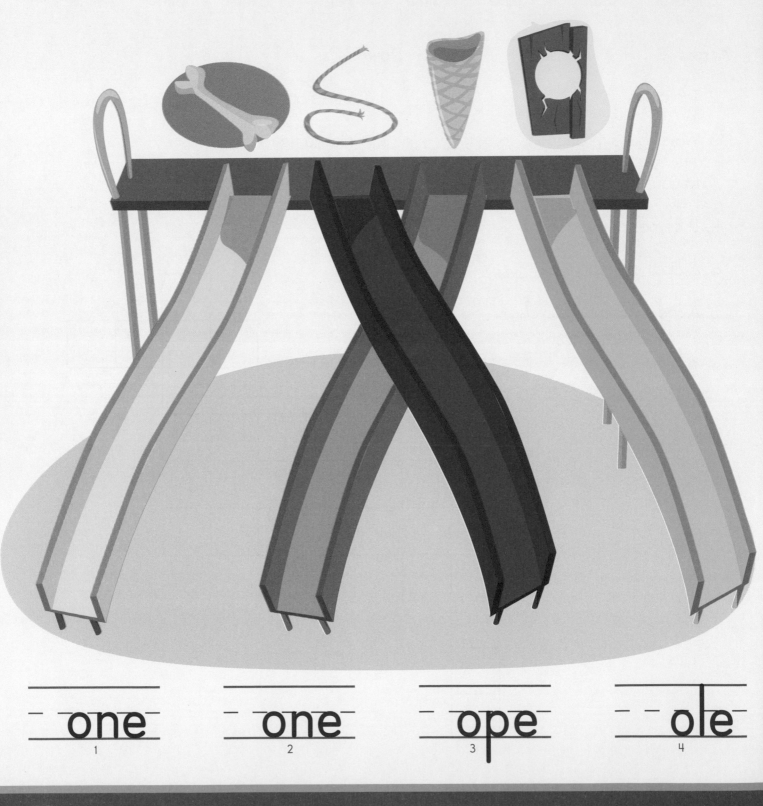

one ____ one ____ ope ____ ole ____
  1   2   3   4

Fast Words

Can you SAY this sentence three times fast? Try it!

The cute duke rode and dozed.

Now WRITE your own sentence. Use these words or other long **o** or long **u** words. Then SAY the sentence three times fast!

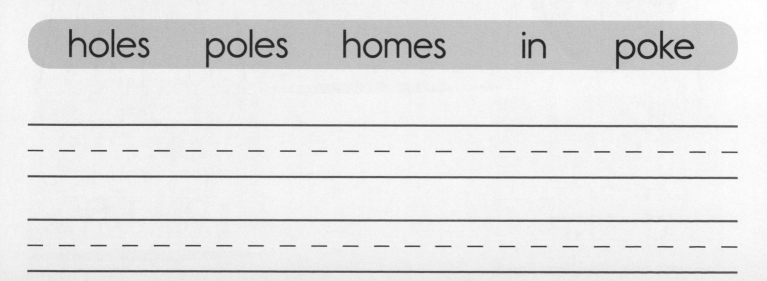

holes   poles   homes   in   poke

Spell Long O and U

Letter Liftoff

FILL IN the vowel for each long **o** or long **u** word.

h__le
1

c__ne
2

r__pe
3

d__ke
4

b__ne
5

Riddle Me This!

UNSCRAMBLE the words in the riddle.

Q: Why did the **kude** put

_____

– – – – – – –

_____

his **neco** on a **erpo?**

_____   _____

– – – – –   – – – – –

_____   _____

A: He wanted to hang onto it!

Opposites Are Everywhere!

FILL IN the word that goes with each picture.

fast or slow?

big or little?

_____

- - - - - - - - - - - - -

1

_____

- - - - - - - - - - - - -

2

_____

- - - - - - - - - - - - -

5

_____

- - - - - - - - - - - - -

6

hot or cold?

short or tall?

_____

- - - - - - - - - - - - -

3

_____

- - - - - - - - - - - - -

4

_____

- - - - - - - - - - - - -

7

_____

- - - - - - - - - - - - -

8

Slide Words

Let's make words that have the letters "c" and "k." DRAW a line between each picture and the ending that matches. Then WRITE the first letter of each word.

_ ey
1

_ up
2

_ at
3

_ ite
4

Letter Liftoff

FILL IN the letter "c" or "k" in each space.

bi _ e
1

_ ave
2

_ ite
3

_ one
4

_ ake
5

Riddle Me This!

UNSCRAMBLE the words to read the riddle.

Q: Why did the **ogd** put two **dils**

_____   _____
- - - - - - -   - - - - - - -

on his **edb**?

_____
- - - - - - -

A: He wanted to sleep under the covers!

Fast Words

Can you SAY this sentence three times fast? Try it!

The bug dug big dog bones.

Now WRITE your own sentence. Use these words or other "b" or "d" words. Then SAY the sentence three times fast!

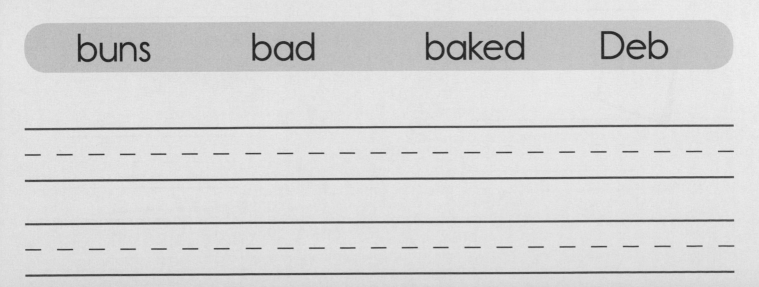

buns   bad   baked   Deb

"B" or "P"?

Travel Tags

Let's make words that have the letters "b" and "p." Then WRITE the words in the tags.

Letter Liftoff

FILL IN the letter "b" or "p" in each space.

ta_ e
1

_ _ ike
2

pi_ e
3

ro_ e
4

_ one
5

"S" or "Z"?

Around We Go!

CIRCLE the things that are spelled with the letter "s."

WRITE the words with "s" on the lines.

_____   _____   _____

_ _ _ _ _ _   _ _ _ _ _ _   _ _ _ _ _ _

_____   _____   _____

Criss Cross

READ the clues. FILL IN the words with "s" or "z" in the boxes.

| doze | hose | maze | nose | rose | size |

Across

4. What _____ shoe do you wear?

5. You can use a _____ to water the flowers.

6. When you take a nap, you _____.

Down

1. A flower that smells nice

2. You can get lost in this.

3. You use this to smell.

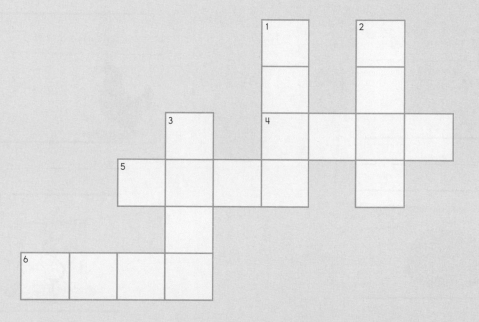

"M" or "N"?

Travel Tags

Let's make words that have the letters "m" and "n." Then WRITE the words in the tags.

Fast Words

Can you SAY this sentence three times fast? Try it!

Nine moms ran nine miles.

Now WRITE your own sentence. Use these words or other "m" or "n" words. Then SAY the sentence three times fast!

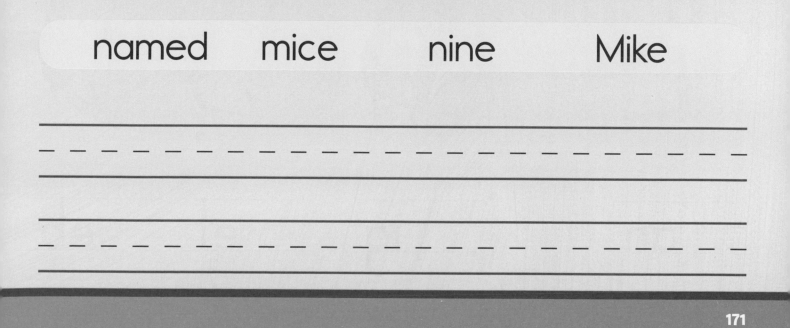

named   mice   nine   Mike

Slide Words

Let's make words that have the letters "v" and "w." DRAW a line between each picture and the ending that matches. Then WRITE the first letter of each word.

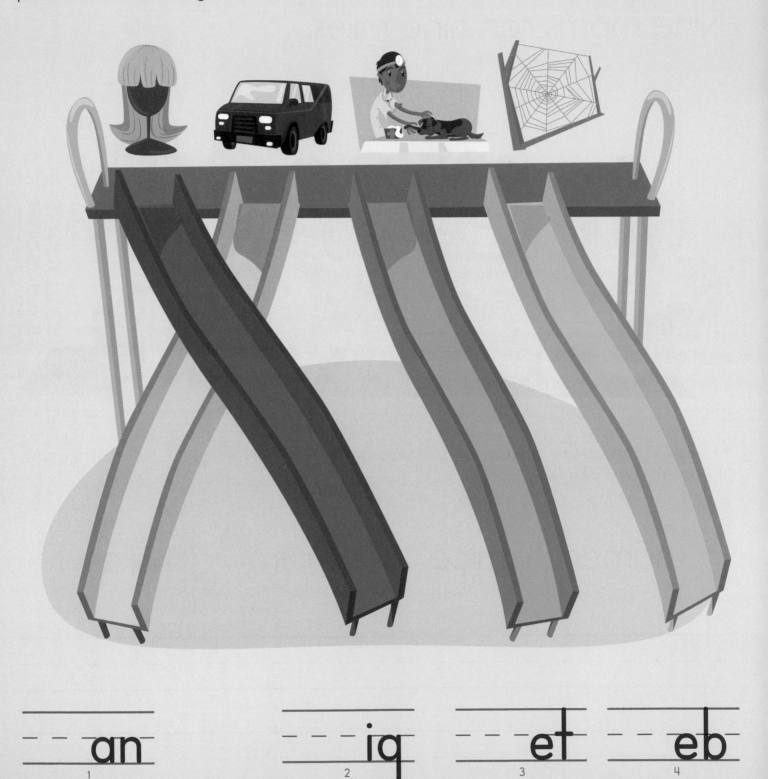

_____ an
1

_____ ig
2

_____ et
3

_____ eb
4

Letter Liftoff

FILL IN the letter "v" or "w" in each space.

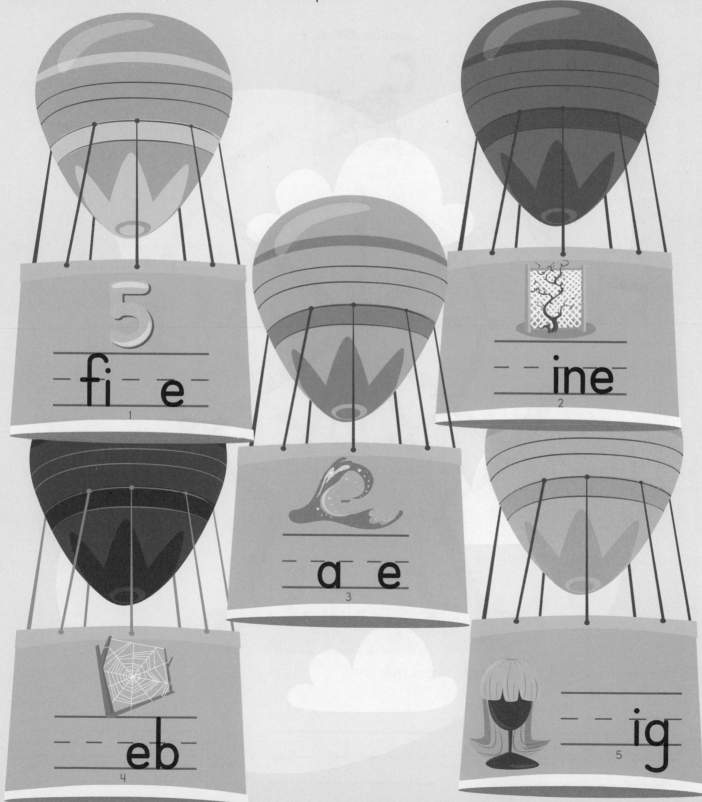

fi_e
1

_ine
2

_a_e
3

_eb
4

_ig
5

"D" or "T"?

Around We Go!

CIRCLE the things that are spelled with the letter "d" or "t."

WRITE the words with "d" and "t" on the lines.

_____   _____   _____

_ _ _ _ _ _ _   _ _ _ _ _ _ _   _ _ _ _ _ _ _

_____   _____   _____

Travel Tags

Let's make words that have the letters "d" and "t." Then WRITE the words in the tags.

Spell with Double Letters

Slide Words

Let's make words that have double letters at the end. DRAW a line between each picture and the ending that matches. Then WRITE the first letter of each word.

ell
1

oll
2

gg
3

iss
4

Fast Words

Can you SAY this sentence three times fast? Try it!

The big bell fell on Bill.

Now WRITE your own sentence. Use these words or other words with double letters. Then SAY the sentence three times fast!

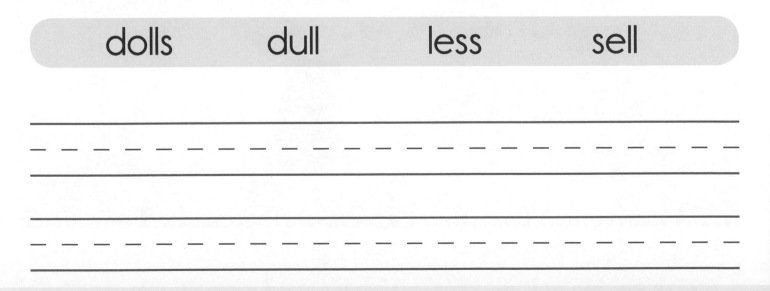

| dolls | dull | less | sell |

_____

- -

_____

- -

_____

What's Happening?

FILL IN the **action** word that goes with each picture.

play or nap?

1

2

jump or stop?

5

6

walk or skate?

3

4

eat or talk?

7

8

Spell with "-Ed" Endings

Slide Words

To make most action words happen in the past, add "-ed." DRAW a line between each picture and the ending that matches. Then WRITE the beginning of each word.

HINT: If a word has a short vowel sound, double the last letter before adding "-ed."
stop → stopped

play   hug   walk   hop

ged   ed   ed   ped
1   2   3   4

Letter Liftoff

FILL IN the ending for each word to make it past tense. If a word has a short vowel sound, be sure to double the last letter before adding "-ed."

HINT: If a word has an "e" at the end, drop the "e" before adding "-ed."

wave
1

hop
2

talk
3

doze
4

hug
5

Spell with "-Ed" Endings

Travel Tags

Let's make more words past tense. DRAW a line from each suitcase to the tag that matches. Then FILL IN the missing endings.

-ed

drop the "e"

play

skate

wave

walk

How Does It End?

The "-ed" endings of these words got chopped off! DRAW a line between the beginning and end of each word. Then WRITE the words in the boxes.

hug   ded

bake   ped

stop   ed

talk   d

nod   ged

miss   ed

_____   _____
- - - - - - - - - - - - - - - -   - - - - - - - - - - - - - - - -
_____   _____

_____   _____
- - - - - - - - - - - - - - - -   - - - - - - - - - - - - - - - -
_____   _____

_____   _____
- - - - - - - - - - - - - - - -   - - - - - - - - - - - - - - - -
_____   _____

Spell with "-Ing" Endings

Letter Liftoff

Sometimes action words end with "-ing." FILL IN the "ing" ending for these words.

eat _____ 1

play _____ 2

walk _____ 3

talk _____ 4

How Does It End?

DRAW a line between the beginning and end of each word. WRITE the words in the boxes.

HINT: If a word has a short vowel sound, double the last letter before adding "-ing": hop → hopping.

run	ning
cut	ping
sit	ting
nap	bing
rub	ping
hop	ting

Spell with "-Ing" Endings

Tricky Endings

Try this trick for making words that end with "-ing." When a word ends with "e," take off the "e" and add "-ing": ride ➜ riding

hide ➜ _____
                  1

rake ➜ _____
                  2

doze ➜ _____
                  3

bite ➜ _____
                  4

tune  _____

_____
5

skate _____

_____
6

dive _____

_____
7

poke _____

_____
8

How Do You Do It?

A word that tells **how** someone does something ends with "-ly." WRITE an "-ly" word on each sign so people know what to do!

Be safe in the water.

Swim _____

Be nice when you talk.

Talk _____

Go for a slow ride.

Ride _____

Fast Words

Can you SAY this sentence three times fast? Try it!

Nate rode slowly and safely.

Now WRITE your own sentence. Use these words or other words with "-ly." Then say the sentence fast!

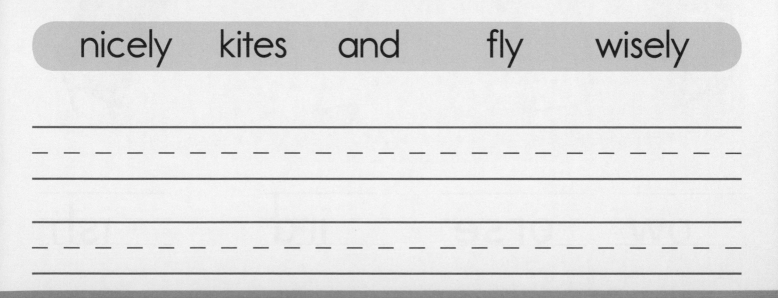

nicely   kites   and   fly   wisely

Spell Animal Words

Slide Words

Let's make animal words. DRAW a line between each picture and the ending that matches. Then WRITE the first letter of each word.

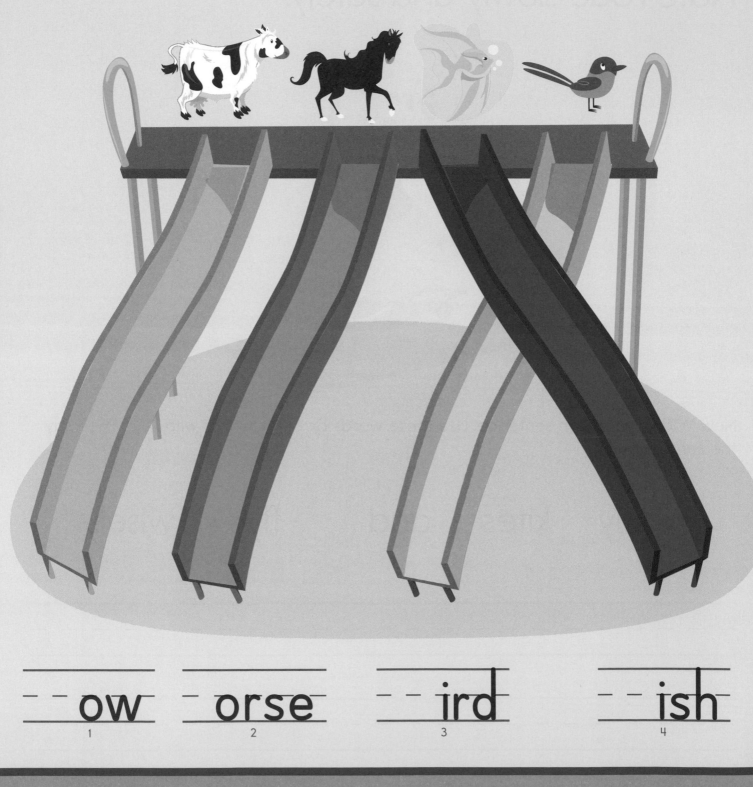

ow   orse   ird   ish

1   2   3   4

Letter Liftoff

FILL IN the beginning letter of each animal word.

_____ nake
1

_____ rog
2

_____ ion
3

_____ ouse
4

_____ oat
5

Spell Plurals

Letter Liftoff

Plural means "more than one." When a word tells about more than one thing, add an "-s": **hat → hats**

WRITE plural words. ADD an "-s" to each word.

bird
1

kite
2

egg
3

bone
4

cat
5

Tricky Endings

If a word ends with "x" or "s," to make it plural, add "-es": **box → boxes**

Try it! WRITE plural words by adding "-es" to these words.

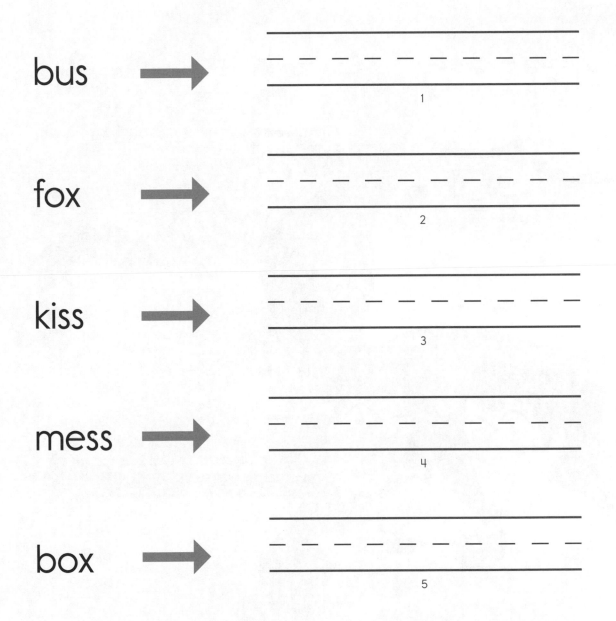

bus → _____
1

fox → _____
2

kiss → _____
3

mess → _____
4

box → _____
5

What Do You See at the Party?

What do you see at Kate's birthday party? FILL IN the blanks using **plural** words.

| cakes | kisses | hats | boxes | cups | buses |

1. There are two pink birthday _____ on the table.

2. The kids are wearing _____ with dots on them.

3. The _____ have presents inside.

4. The blue _____ are on the table too.

5. Tim is playing with yellow toy _____.

6. Kate's mother and father are giving her _____ _____ .

People Words with "-Er"

Getting to Know You

Some words that end with "-er" tell about people. WRITE the word that matches each person.

eater	jumper	kisser	talker	walker

_____
- - - - - - - - - - - - - - - - - -
_____
1

_____
- - - - - - - - - - - - - - - - - -
_____
2

_____
- - - - - - - - - - - - - - - - - -
_____
3

_____
- - - - - - - - - - - - - - - - - -
_____
4

_____
- - - - - - - - - - - - - - - - - -
_____
5

What Do You Do?

WRITE "-er" words that tell about these people.

HINT: When a word ends with an "e," drop the "e" before adding "-er."

1. If you **bake** a cake, you are a _____.

2. If you work in a **mine**, you are a _____.

3. If you ride your **bike**, you are a _____.

4. If you like to **skate**, you are a _____.

5. If you **rope** cows, you are a _____.

6. If you **dive** into the water, you are a _____.

People Words with "-Er"

How Does It End?

DRAW a line between each word and its "-er" ending. WRITE the words in the boxes.

HINT: When a word has a short vowel sound, double the last letter before adding "-er."

swim   ger

hop   per

win   ner

sit   mer

hug   ter

nap   per

Criss Cross

READ the clues. FILL IN the people words in the boxes.

| teacher | baker | eater | talker | diver | digger | skater |

Across

2. A person who bakes cakes

3. He likes to skate.

4. A person who digs

6. Someone who teaches

Down

1. A person who talks and talks

4. She dives into the pool.

5. Someone who eats

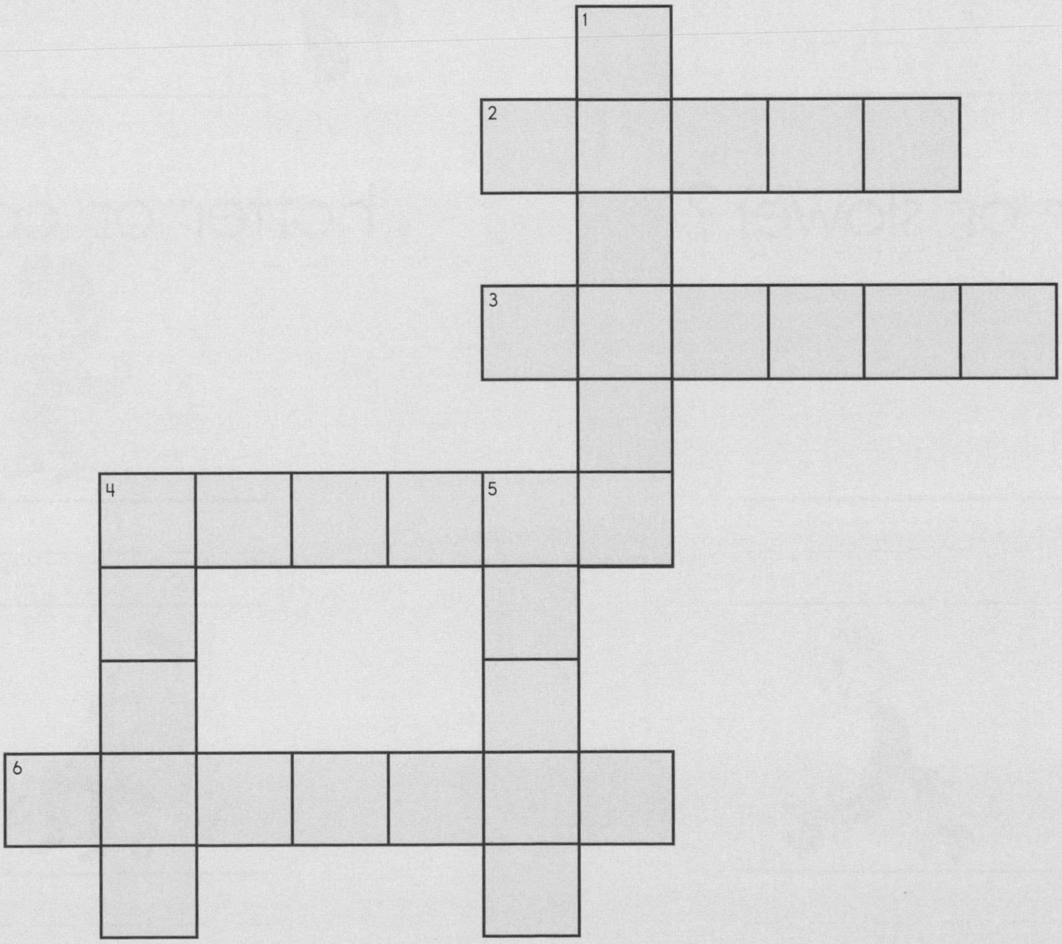

Comparing Words

Look and Compare

Add "-er" at the end of describing words to compare two things. WRITE the "-er" word that tells about each person or animal.

bigger or smaller?

_____
_____
1

_____
_____
2

shorter or taller?

_____
_____
5

_____
_____
6

faster or slower?

_____
_____
3

_____
_____
4

hotter or colder?

_____
_____
7

_____
_____
8

Compare the Racers

Add "-est" at the end of a describing word when you compare more than two things.
FILL IN the "-est" word that tells about each car in the race.

| slowest | fastest | biggest | smallest | hottest | wettest |

Letter Liftoff

Who are these people? FILL IN the first letter of each word.

__ aby
1

__ irl
2

__ oy
3

__ an
4

__ ady
5

Criss Cross

READ the clues. FILL IN the people words in the boxes.

mother   boys   sister   man   baby   girl   father

Across

2. The opposite of *girls* is _____.

5. Another word for *dad* is _____.

6. Another word for *mom* is _____.

Down

1. A _____ is very little.

3. The opposite of *brother* is _____.

4. A _____ will grow up to be a lady.

6. Your father is a _____.

Alphabet Soup

Use the letters in the soup to WRITE the words to match the pictures. CROSS OUT each letter in the soup after you use it.

c e o z
n e m a h
e k o s
a r e

1

2

3

4

Bubble Pop

LOOK at the words in the bubbles. CROSS OUT the words that are misspelled.

stoped

talkng

rakd

raked

hiding

slowley

hideing

talking

slowly

stopped

Answers

Page 114
1. ram
2. cat
3. map
4. fan

Page 115
Suggestion: The man and the ram ran.

Page 116
1. ram
2. rat
3. hat
4. bat

Page 117

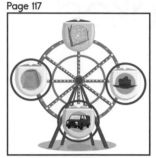

hat, van, bag

Page 118
1. The ram eats a **yam**.
2. The fan cools the **man**.
3. The hat is on the **cat**.

Page 119
Suggestions: bag, bat, cat, gab, gas, rag, rat, sag, sat, tab, tag

Page 120
1. pen
2. leg
3. bed
4. vet

Page 121
1. hen
2. bed
3. ten
4. pen
5. net

Page 122

web, hen, pen

Page 123
Suggestion: Red beds have red legs.

Page 124
1. The wet pet saw the **vet**.
2. The hen has a **pen**.
3. The bed was **red**.

Page 125
Suggestions: bed, bet, den, jet, men, met, net, ten, Jeb, Jed, Deb, Ted, Ned

Pages 126–127
1. one
2. two
3. three
4. four
5. five
6. six
7. seven
8. eight

Page 128
1. six
2. wig
3. bib
4. pin

Page 129

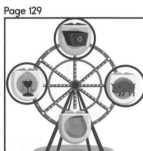

wig, bin, pig

Page 130
Suggestion: Pigs dig big kids.

Page 131
1. dig
2. pig
3. pin
4. bin

Page 132
1. The pig lost her **wig**.
2. My pin fell in the **bin**.
3. "Help me dig," said the **pig**.

Page 133
Suggestions: big, bin, bit, nib, nip, nit, pig, pin, pit, tip, tin, wig, win, wit

Page 134
1. dog
2. box
3. pot
4. mop

Page 135
1. pot
2. dot
3. dog
4. log

Page 136
1. The dog jumps on a **log**.
2. The box is on top of the **fox**.
3. Can you hop over the **top**?

Page 137
Suggestion: The fox mops a box.

Page 138
Suggestions: dog, dot, god, got, hog, hop, hot, mop, pod, pot, top, Tom

Page 139
Q. What **dog** pops out of a **pot** that is **hot**?

Page 140
1. cup
2. bus
3. sun
4. tub

Page 141
1. The cub jumped in the **tub**.
2. The pup found a **cup**.
3. The bug hid under the **rug**.

Page 142

cup, duck, sun

Page 143
Q: Why did the **bug** drive his **bus** into the **tub**?
Note: *bus* or *sub* works, but *bus* matches the picture.

Page 144
Suggestions: bug, bum, bun, bus, gum, gun, Gus, mug, rub, rug, run, sub, sum, sun

Page 145

ACROSS	DOWN
1. hut	2. tub
3. bus	4. sun
5. bug	5. but
7. nut	6. gum
8. mud	

Pages 146–147
1. green
2. blue
3. brown
4. red
5. yellow
6. white
7. purple
8. orange

Page 148
1. cake
2. gate
3. wave
4. cane

Page 149
1. wave
2. cave
3. cane
4. cape

Page 150

rake, cake, lake

Page 151
Suggestion: Safe waves save lakes.

Page 152
1. vine
2. Pete
3. kite
4. bike

Page 153
1. Pete
2. pipe
3. bike
4. kite
5. nine

Page 154
Suggestion: Pete piled wide tiles.

Page 155

ACROSS	DOWN
2. dime	1. kite
3. pipe	3. Pete
4. nine	6. bite
5. time	
6. bike	

Page 156
1. bone
2. cone
3. rope
4. hole

Page 157
Suggestion: Poles poke holes in homes.

Page 158
1. hole
2. cone
3. rope
4. duke
5. bone

Page 159
Q: Why did the **duke** put his **cone** on a **rope**?

Pages 160–161
1. fast
2. slow
3. cold
4. hot
5. big
6. little
7. tall
8. short

Answers

Page 162
1. key
2. cup
3. cat
4. kite

Page 163
1. bike
2. cave
3. kite
4. cone
5. cake

Page 164
Q: Why did the **dog** put two **lids** on his **bed**?

Page 165
Suggestion: Deb baked bad buns.

Page 166
b: tub, bib, web
p: map, cup, pot

Page 167
1. tape
2. bike
3. pipe
4. rope
5. bone

Page 168

hose, bus, nose

Page 169
ACROSS   DOWN
4. size   1. rose
5. hose   2. maze
6. doze   3. nose

Page 170
m: map, dime, ham
n: nut, hen, vine

Page 171
Suggestion: Mike named nine mice.

Page 172
1. van
2. wig
3. vet
4. web

Page 173
1. five
2. vine
3. wave
4. web
5. wig

Page 174

bed, cat, top

Page 175
d: dive, dime, bed
t: tape, kite, net

Page 176
1. bell
2. doll
3. egg
4. kiss

Page 177
Suggestion: Dull dolls sell less.

Pages 178-179
1. nap
2. play
3. walk
4. skate
5. stop
6. jump
7. eat
8. talk

Page 180
1. hugged
2. played
3. walked
4. hopped

Page 181
1. waved
2. hopped
3. talked
4. dozed
5. hugged

Page 182
-ed: played, walked
Drop the "e": waved skated

Page 183
hugged, baked, stopped, talked, nodded, missed

Page 184
1. eating
2. playing
3. walking
4. talking

Page 185
running, cutting, sitting, napping, rubbing, hopping

Pages 186-187
1. hide →hiding
2. rake →raking
3. doze →dozing
4. bite →biting
5. tune →tuning
6. skate →skating
7. dive →diving
8. poke →poking

Page 188
1. Swim **Safely**
2. Talk **Nicely**
3. Ride **Slowly**

Page 189
Suggestion: Fly kites nicely and wisely.

Page 190
1. cow
2. horse
3. bird
4. fish

Page 191
1. snake
2. frog
3. lion
4. mouse
5. goat

Page 192
1. birds
2. kites
3. eggs
4. bones
5. cats

Page 193
1. buses
2. foxes
3. kisses
4. messes
5. boxes

Pages 194-195
1. cakes
2. hats
3. boxes
4. cups
5. buses
6. kisses

Page 196
1. eater
2. jumper
3. walker
4. kisser
5. talker

Page 197
1. baker
2. miner
3. biker
4. skater
5. roper
6. diver

Page 198
swimmer, hopper, winner, sitter, hugger, napper

Page 199
ACROSS   DOWN
2. baker   1. talker
3. skater   4. diver
4. digger   5. eater
6. teacher

Page 200
1. bigger
2. smaller
3. slower
4. faster
5. shorter
6. taller
7. colder
8. hotter

Page 201
1. biggest
2. slowest
3. smallest
4. hottest
5. wettest
6. fastest

Page 202
1. baby
2. girl
3. boy
4. man
5. lady

Page 203
ACROSS   DOWN
2. boys   1. baby
5. father   3. sister
6. mother   4. girl
          6. man

Page 204
1. cone
2. rake
3. hose
4. maze

Page 205
Misspelled words: hideing, stoped, slowley, rakd, talkng

1st Grade
Vocabulary Puzzles

Read and Trace

READ the words and TRACE them. Do you know what they mean?

body

nose

teeth

finger

bone

Picture Pointers

WRITE the word for each picture clue in the grid.

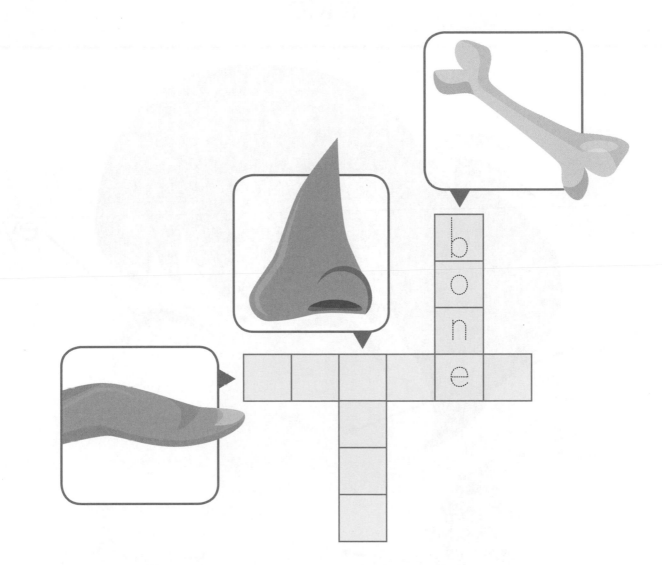

b
o
n
e

Draw It

Help finish the picture! DRAW parts of the face to match the words.

face

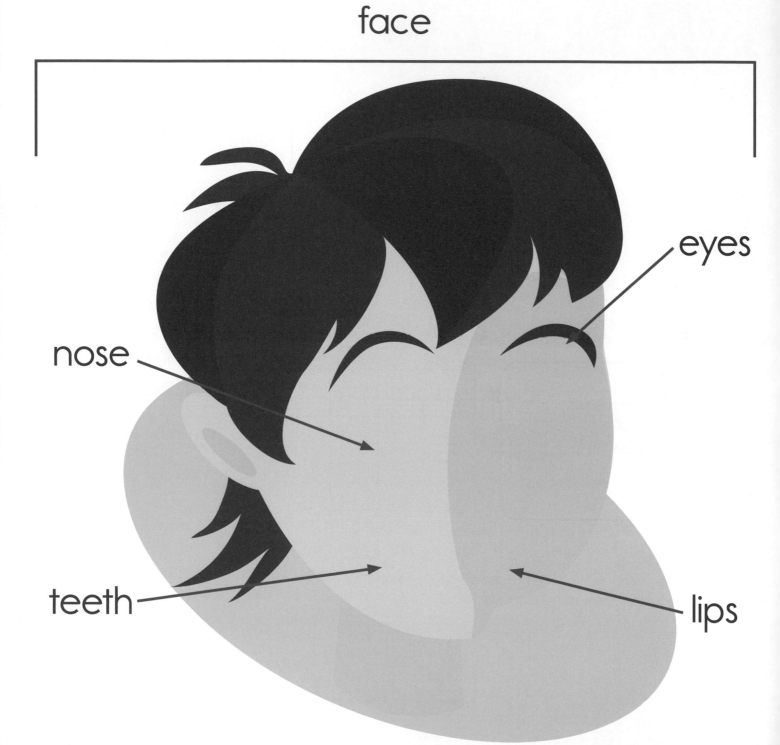

eyes

nose

teeth

lips

Maze Crazy!

DRAW a line through the words for **body parts** to get to the boy. START at the yellow arrow.

Family Tree

Read and Trace

READ the words and TRACE them. Do you know what they mean?

family

father

mother

daughter

son

Match the Meaning

DRAW a line to match the word with its picture.

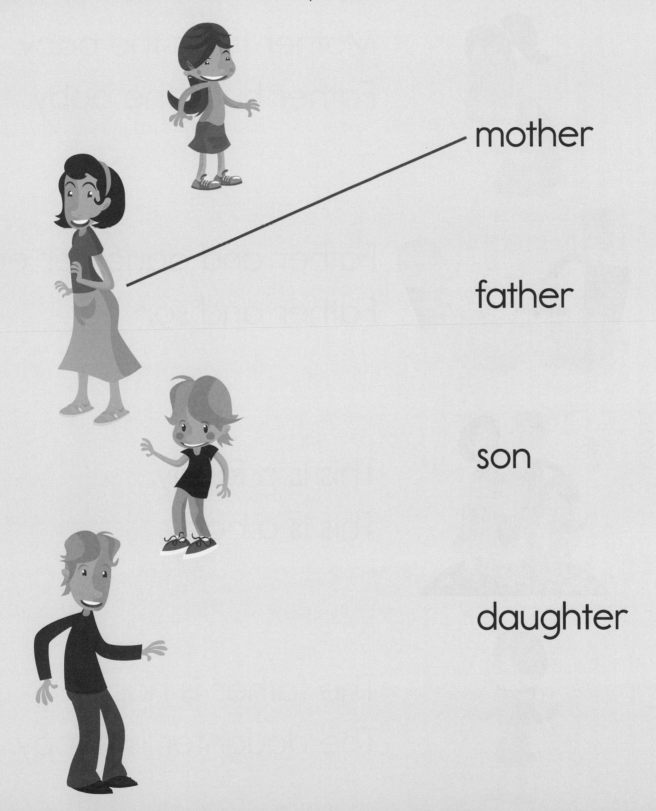

mother

father

son

daughter

Family Tree

Right or Wrong?

UNDERLINE the sentence that matches the picture.

1.

   Mother hugs the baby.

   Father hugs the baby.

2.

   Father and daughter eat.

   Father and son eat.

3.

   This is a family.

   This is a body.

4.

   The father is happy.

   The daughter is happy.

Word Pictures

COLOR the spaces that show words for FAMILY.

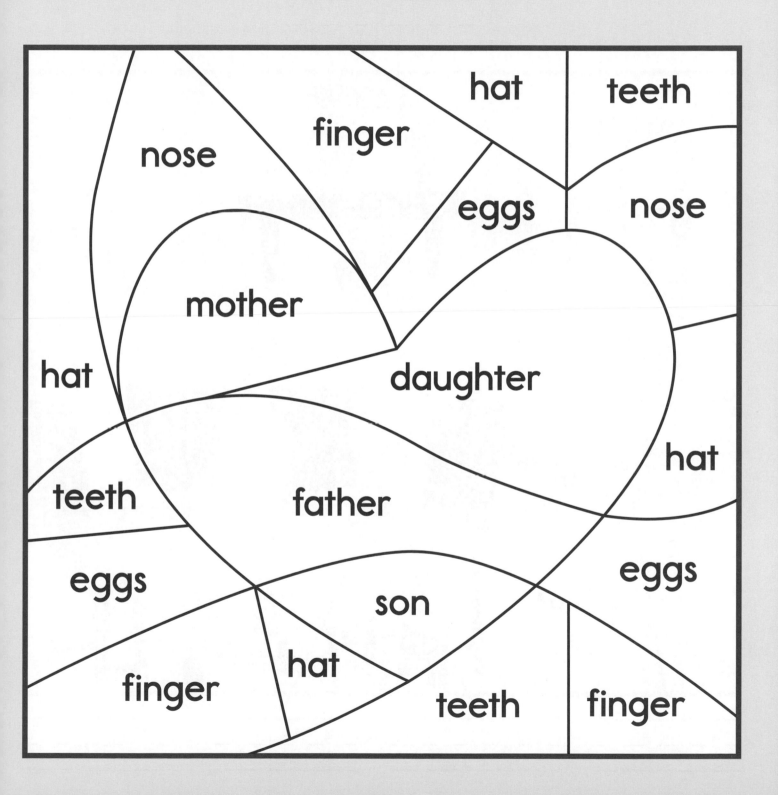

What's Cooking?

Read and Trace

READ the words and TRACE them. Do you know what they mean?

kitchen

stove   spoon   knife   fork

Blank Out

FINISH each sentence with a word from the word box. CROSS OUT the words as you use them.

kitchen	knife	spoon	fork	stove

1. The _____ gets hot.

2. A _____ cuts food.

3. I eat ice cream with a _____.

4. The _____ is a room in

   our house.

5. You eat with a knife, a spoon,

   and a _____.

What's Cooking?

Draw It!

Help finish the picture! DRAW things to match the words.

juice

food

fork   knife   spoon

Cross Out

CROSS OUT things that **don't** go in the **kitchen**.

Put It On!

Read and Trace

READ the words and TRACE them. Do you know what they mean?

Picture Pointers

WRITE the word for each picture clue in the grid.

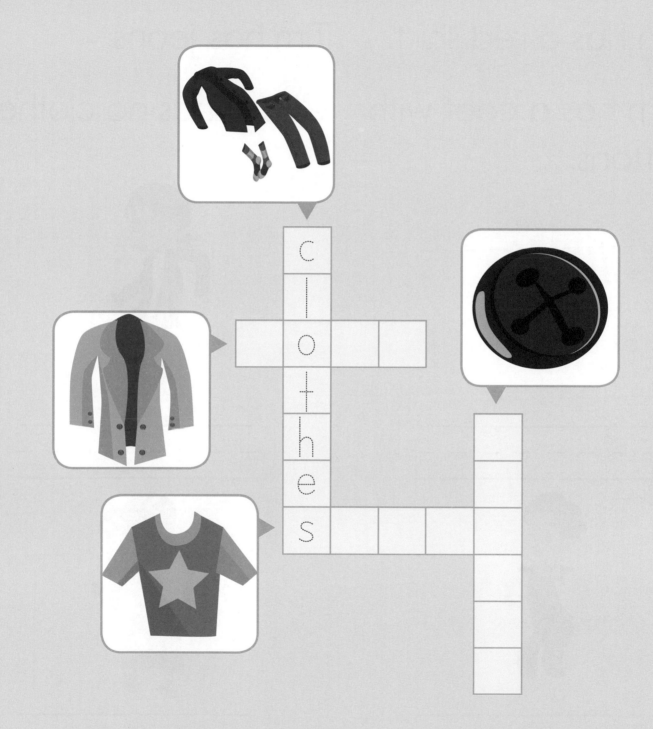

Put It On!

Find the Friend

READ the clues. Then WRITE the friend's name under each picture.

Ken has a red shirt.

Pam has a coat with buttons.

Tim has jeans.

Chuck has no clothes!

_____

- - - - - - - - - - - -

_____

_____

- - - - - - - - - - - -

_____

Hide and Seek

CIRCLE the clothes in the picture.

What Do You Do?

Read and Trace

Things you do are called **actions**. TRACE the action words in the sentences below.

You _wear_ clothes.

You _wash_ dishes.

You _cook_ at the stove.

You _drink_ juice.

You _visit_ friends.

Match the Meaning

The pictures below are in need of action! DRAW a line to match the action word with the right picture.

wear

wash

cook

drink

visit

What Do You Do?

Circle It

CIRCLE the words that are actions.

1. eat   run   stove   red

2. baby   play   wash   cake

3. wear   leg   green   hug

4. visit   nose   cook   kitchen

Right or Wrong?

UNDERLINE the sentence that matches the picture.

1. I drink my hands.

   I wash my hands.

2. I visit my granny.

   I cook my granny.

3. I wear my mittens.

   I wash my mittens.

4. Bob visits juice.

   Bob drinks juice.

How Do You Feel?

Read and Trace

READ the words about feelings and TRACE them. Do you know what they mean?

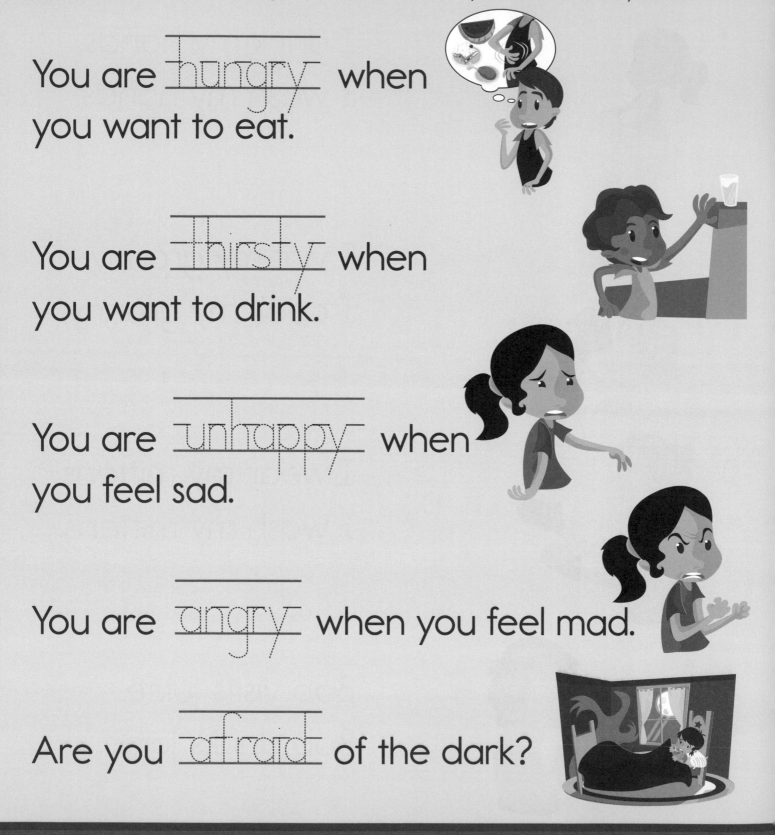

You are hungry when you want to eat.

You are thirsty when you want to drink.

You are unhappy when you feel sad.

You are angry when you feel mad.

Are you afraid of the dark?

Draw It!

Help finish the picture! DRAW parts of the face to match the words.

HINT: Is a girl who is unhappy smiling or frowning?

unhappy

angry

afraid

happy

Circle It

CIRCLE the words that are feelings.

1. wash   sad   daughter   angry

2. shirt   clothes   afraid   happy

3. drink   fork   knife   thirsty

4. hungry   body   mad   son

Match the Meaning

DRAW a line to match the words that have the same meaning.

afraid   sad

unhappy   scared

angry   nap

drink   mad

sleep   sip

Animals

Read and Trace

READ the words and TRACE them. Do you know what they mean?

Draw It

Help finish the pictures! COLOR or DRAW the pictures to match the sentences.

The leopard is yellow.

The kangaroo is red.

The gorilla wears a hat.

The penguin has a blue belly.

Animals

Match the Meaning

DRAW a line to match the word with its picture.

walrus

penguin

kangaroo

gorilla

Word Pictures

COLOR the spaces that show words for **animals**.

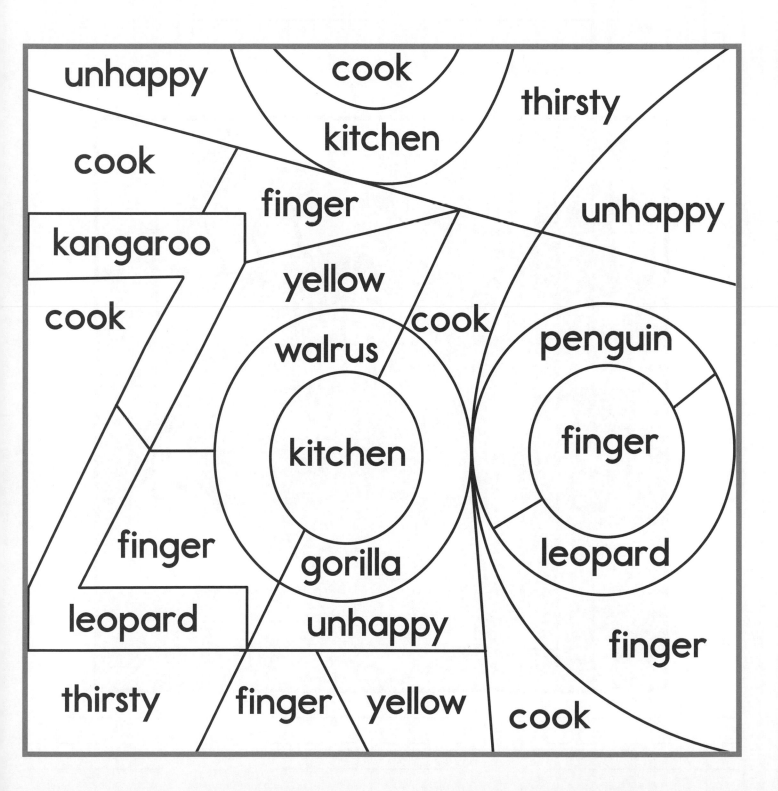

unhappy · cook · kitchen · thirsty · cook · finger · unhappy · kangaroo · yellow · cook · walrus · cook · penguin · kitchen · finger · finger · gorilla · leopard · leopard · unhappy · finger · thirsty · finger · yellow · cook

At the Zoo

Read and Trace

READ the words and TRACE them. Do you know what they mean?

cage   balloon

pigeon   skates   pool

Yes or No?

LOOK at the picture. READ the questions about Tara. CIRCLE YES or NO to answer.

1. Does Tara have a balloon?   YES   NO

2. Is Tara in a cage?   YES   NO

3. Is there a walrus on Tara's shirt? YES   NO

4. Is Tara in a pool?   YES   NO

5. Is Tara wearing skates?   YES   NO

Picture Pointers

WRITE the word for each picture clue in the grid.

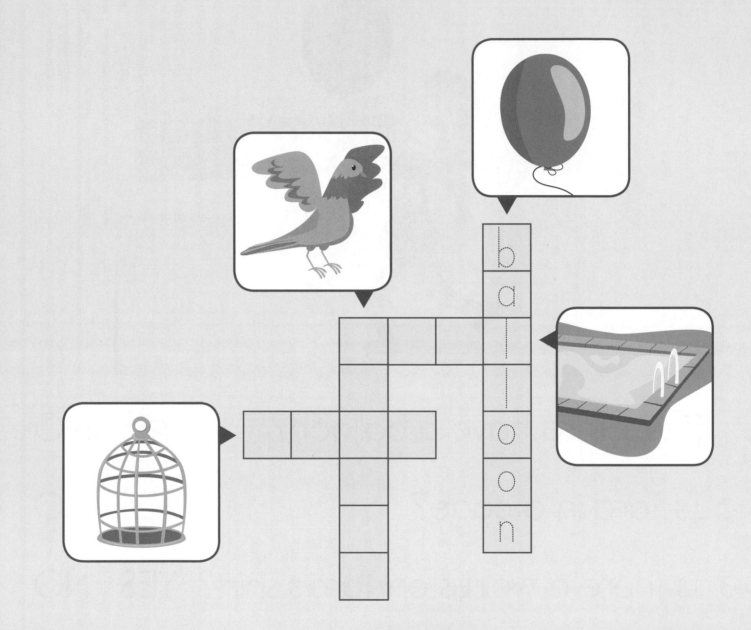

Draw It

Help finish the pictures! COLOR or DRAW the pictures to match the sentences.

The balloon is green.

The penguin is in a cage.

The pigeon wears skates.

There is a red fish in the pool.

Animal Actions

Read and Trace

READ the words and TRACE them. Do you know what they mean?

The gorilla swings in the tree.

The walrus floats in the pool.

The leopard hides in his cage.

The monkey climbs up.

The elephant escapes from the zoo.

Right or Wrong?

UNDERLINE the sentence that matches the picture.

1. The balloon floats in the air.
The balloon hides in the air.

2.  I float the tree.
I climb the tree.

3.  The baby kangaroo is hiding.
The baby kangaroo is swinging.

4.  The pigeon escapes.
The pigeon swings.

Circle It

CIRCLE the words that are actions.

1. penguin   hide   hungry   see

2. drink   juice   kitchen   wear

3. swings   shoes   floats   bone

4. escape   pigeon   jeans   climb

Find the Friend

READ the clues. Then WRITE the friend's name under each picture.

Jan swings in
the yard.

Molly hides under
her bed.

Taj escapes from
the dog.

Bill floats in the pool.

_____

- - - - - - - - - -

_____

_____

- - - - - - - - - -

_____

_____

- - - - - - - - - -

_____

What Do You See?

Read and Trace

READ the words and TRACE them. Do you know what they mean?

I see sharp teeth.

I see a young kangaroo.

I see a colorful bird.

I see a dry dog.

I see a silly face.

Match the Meaning

CIRCLE the picture that matches the word.

1. sharp

2. dry

3. young

4. colorful

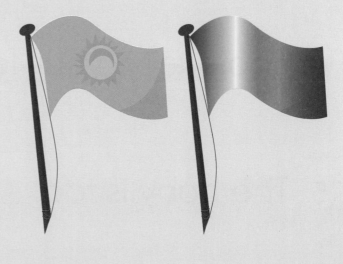

What Do You See?

Blank Out

FINISH each sentence with a word from the word box. CROSS OUT the words as you use them.

> dry   young   sharp   silly   colorful

1. When I feel _____, I giggle a lot.

2. A knife is very _____.

3. I like to draw _____ pictures.

4. Boots keep your feet _____ in the rain.

5. The baby is too _____ to walk.

Night and Day

Opposites are two words that mean very different things, like *wet* and *dry*.

DRAW a line to match each word under the moon to its opposite under the sun.

wet	colorful
unhappy	dry
hot	cold
young	happy
gray	old

Yours, Mine, and Ours

Read and Trace

If something **belongs** to you, then you own it. READ the words and TRACE them. Do you know what they mean?

HINT: When you use someone's name, you need to use a punctuation mark called an *apostrophe* before the "s."

Who does the balloon _belong_ to?

The balloon is _mine_.

It is _my_ balloon.

The skates are _his_.

The spoon is _hers_.

The puppy is <u>ours</u>.

It is <u>our</u> puppy.

That is Wanda<u>'s</u> chair.

That coat is <u>yours</u>.

It is <u>your</u> coat.

Yours, Mine, and Ours

Blank Out

FINISH each sentence with a word from the word box. CROSS OUT the words as you use them.

his	her	mine	ours	yours

1. That toy belongs to me. It is _____.

2. Give this ball to Jake. It is _____.

3. That candy belongs to you. It is _____.

4. Tara wants _____ bag back.

5. We made that picture. It is _____.

Match the Meaning

DRAW a line to match the words that **belong** together.

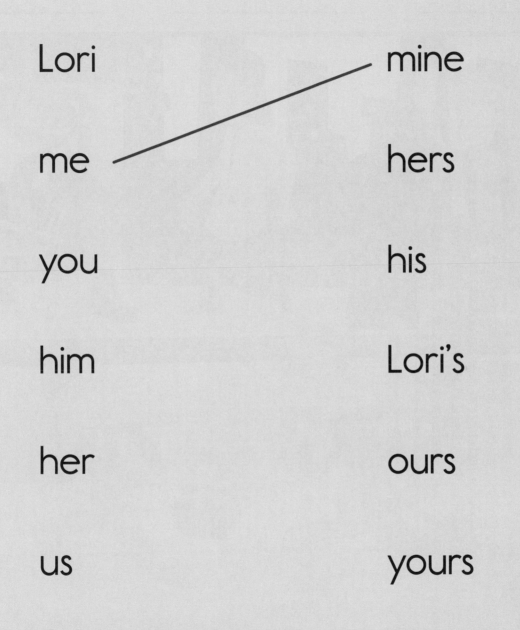

Lori	mine
me	hers
you	his
him	Lori's
her	ours
us	yours

People

Read and Trace

READ the words and TRACE them. Do you know what they mean?

mailman   doctor   teacher

policeman   burglar

Match the Meaning

DRAW a line to match the word with its picture.

policeman

burglar

doctor

mailman

Blank Out

FINISH each sentence with a word from the word box. CROSS OUT the words as you use them.

| teacher | people | policeman |
| mailman | doctor | |

1. You see lots of _____ on the street every day.

2. I go to my _____ when I am sick.

3. The _____ brings our mail every day.

4. You find a _____ in school.

5. A _____ will catch the burglar.

Hide and Seek

LOOK at the words in the word box. CIRCLE these **people** in the picture. CROSS OUT the words as you find them.

| policeman | mother | mailman | father |

Places to See

Read and Trace

READ the words and TRACE them. Do you know what they mean?

playground   bridge   building

station   market

Picture Pointers

WRITE the word for each picture clue in the grid.

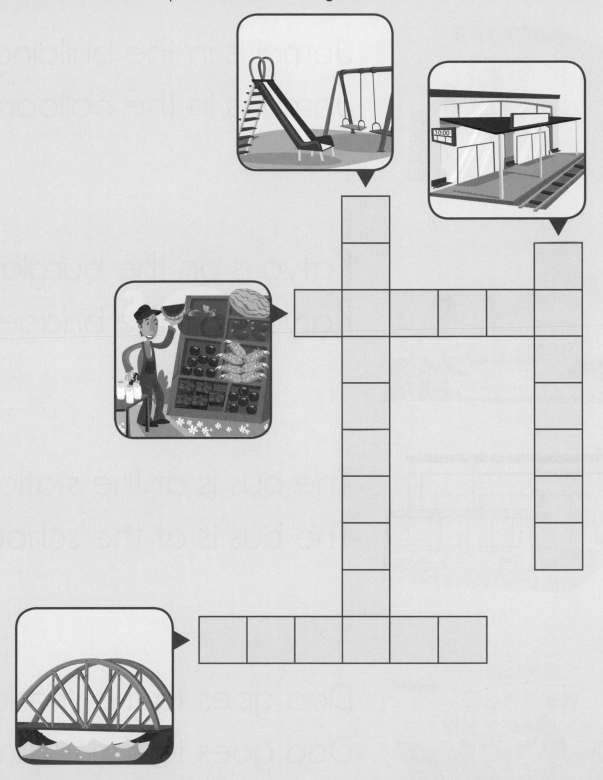

Right or Wrong?

UNDERLINE the sentence that matches the picture.

1.

Jamal is in the building.

Jamal is in the balloon.

2.

Katya is on the burglar.

Katya is on the bridge.

3.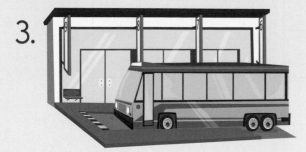

The bus is at the station.

The bus is at the school.

4.

Dad goes to the market.

Dad goes to the mailman.

Word Pictures

COLOR the spaces that show words for **places**.

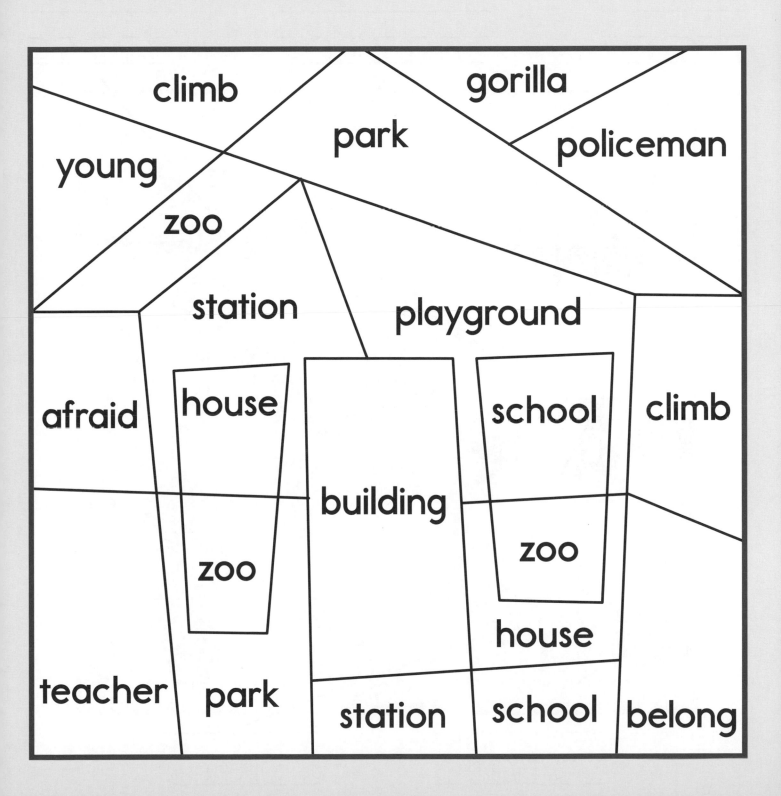

Read and Trace

READ the words and TRACE them. Do you know what they mean?

boat   airplane   taxi

wheel   bike

Match the Meaning

DRAW a line to match the word with its picture.

airplane

taxi

boat

bike

Draw It

Help finish the pictures! DRAW or COLOR the things that go to match the sentences.

The airplane has two wheels.

The taxi is yellow.

The bike has blue wheels.

The boat has green spots on it.

Cross Out

CROSS OUT things that **don't** have **wheels**.

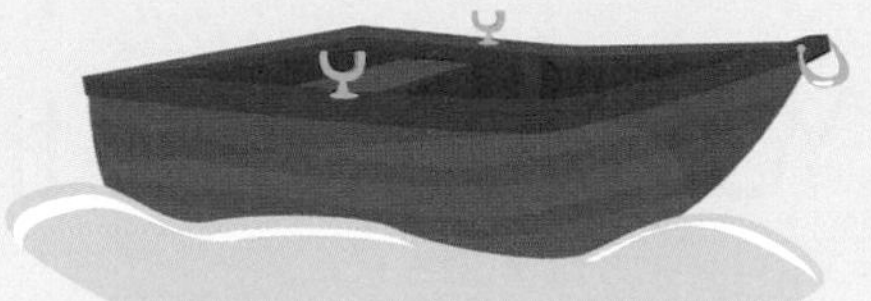

People Actions

Read and Trace

READ the words and TRACE them. Do you know what they mean?

You ~bite~ the hot dog.

You ~chase~ the puppy.

You ~listen~ to your mother.

You ~dance~ to the music.

You ~speak~ to your father.

Blank Out

FINISH each sentence with a word from the word box. CROSS OUT the words as you use them.

bite   chase   listen   dance   speak

1. You have to _____ if you want to hear.

2. I have a doll that can _____ . She says "Mama!"

3. My dog will _____ any cat he sees.

4. Mom likes to _____ on her toes.

5. I don't like it when bugs _____ me.

Circle It

CIRCLE the words that are **actions**.

1. family   wear   clothes   visit

2. balloon   swing   escape   pigeon

3. bite   truck   chase   airplane

4. doctor   listen   yours   dance

Right or Wrong?

UNDERLINE the sentence that matches the picture.

1.

The dog climbs the bone.

The dog bites the bone.

2.

I speak on the phone.

I swing on the phone.

3.

Rudy chases the ball.

Rudy climbs the ball.

4.

Bella dances on the rug.

Bella drinks on the rug.

Where Is It?

Read and Trace

READ the words and TRACE them. Do you know what they mean? Where is Doggo?

between the buildings

across the street

beside the stove

below the bridge

inside the cage

Draw It

Help finish the picture! COLOR the picture to match the sentences.

The blue balloon is beside the green balloon.

The red balloon is between the yellow balloons.

The orange balloon is below the yellow balloon.

There is a star inside the orange balloon.

Night and Day

DRAW a line to match each word under the moon to its opposite under the sun.

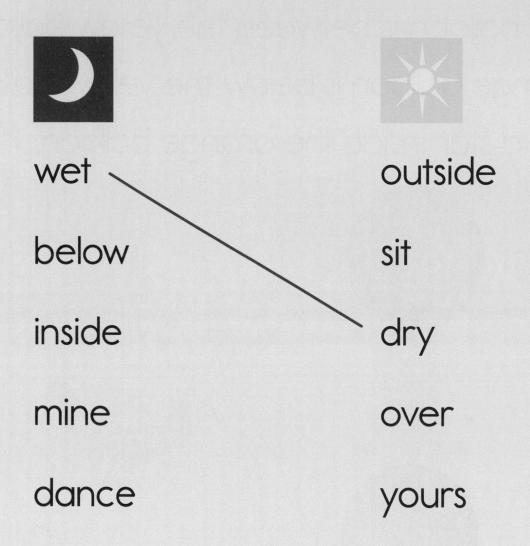

wet	outside
below	sit
inside	dry
mine	over
dance	yours

Find the Friend

READ the clues. Then WRITE the friend's name under each house.

Sasha lives beside Nanci.

Aja lives across the street from Waldo.

Maria lives inside the red house.

Fred lives between Aja and Maria.

It's Time for Time

Read and Trace

READ the words and TRACE them. Do you know what they mean?

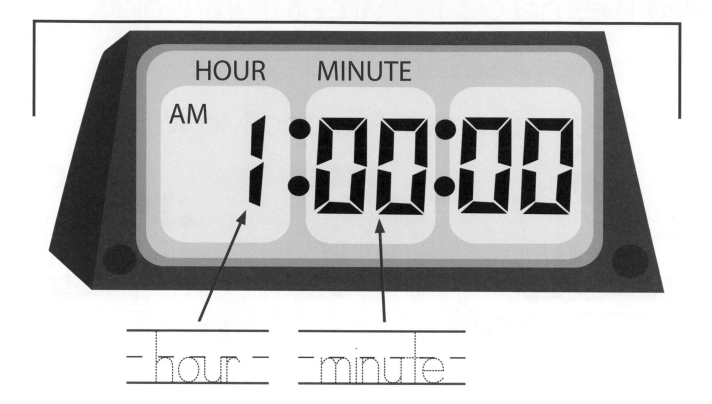

1 day = 24 hours

1 hour = 60 minutes

What time is it on your clock? _____

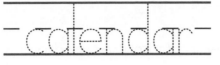

calendar

year

JANUARY						
S	M	T	W	T	F	S
					1	2	3
4	5	6	7	8	9	10
11	12	13	14	15	16	17
18	19	20	21	22	23	24
25	26	27	28	29	30	31

FEBRUARY						
S	M	T	W	T	F	S
1	2	3	4	5	6	7
8	9	10	11	12	13	14
15	16	17	18	19	20	21
22	23	24	25	26	27	28

MARCH						
S	M	T	W	T	F	S
1	2	3	4	5	6	7
8	9	10	11	12	13	14
15	16	17	18	19	20	21
22	23	24	25	26	27	28
29	30	31				

APRIL						
S	M	T	W	T	F	S
			1	2	3	4
5	6	7	8	9	10	11
12	13	14	15	16	17	18
19	20	21	22	23	24	25
26	27	28	29	30		

MAY						
S	M	T	W	T	F	S
					1	2
3	4	5	6	7	8	9
10	11	12	13	14	15	16
17	18	19	20	21	22	23
24	25	26	27	28	29	30
31						

JUNE						
S	M	T	W	T	F	S
	1	2	3	4	5	6
7	8	9	10	11	12	13
14	15	16	17	18	19	20
21	22	23	24	25	26	27
28	29	30				

JULY						
S	M	T	W	T	F	S
		1		3	4	
5	6	7	8	9	10	11
12	13	14	15	16	17	18
19	20	21	22	23	24	25
26	27	28	29	30	31	

AUGUST						
S	M	T	W	T	F	S
						1
2	3	4	5	6	7	8
9	10	11	12	13	14	15
16	17	18	19	20	21	22
23	24	25	26	27	28	29
30	31					

SEPTEMBER						
S	M	T	W	T	F	S
		1	2	3	4	5
6	7	8	9	10	11	12
13	14	15	16	17	18	19
20	21	22	23	24	25	26
27	28	29	30			

OCTOBER						
S	M	T	W	T	F	S
				1	2	3
4	5	6	7	8	9	10
11	12	13	14	15	16	17
18	19	20	21	22	23	24
25	26	27	28	29	30	31

NOVEMBER						
S	M	T	W	T	F	S
1	2	3	4	5	6	7
8	9	10	11	12	13	14
15	16	17	18	19	20	21
22	23	24	25	26	27	28
29	30					

DECEMBER						
S	M	T	W	T	F	S
		1	2	3	4	5
6	7	8	9	10	11	12
13	14	15	16	17	18	19
20	21	22	23	24	25	26
27	28	29	30	31		

month

date

7 days = 1 week

12 months = 1 year

What is today's date?

It's Time for Time

Blank Out!

FINISH each sentence with a word from the word box. CROSS OUT the words as you use them.

| year | month | clock | calendar | hour |

1. Use the _____ to see the time.

2. There are 60 minutes in an _____.

3. Lia's birthday is in the _____ of April.

4. The _____ shows the days of the week.

5. There are 12 months in a _____.

Right or Wrong?

UNDERLINE the sentence that matches the picture.

1.
It will be 9:52 in one hour.
It will be 9:52 in one month.

2.
Next month it will be 2012.
Next year it will be 2012.

3.
May 15 is the date of the party.
May 15 is the month of the party.

4.
It will be 10:05 in five minutes.
It will be 10:05 in five hours.

Days of the Week

Read and Trace

READ the words and TRACE them.
Do you know what they mean?

JULY						
S	M	T	W	T	F	S
			1	2	3	4
5	6	7	8	9	10	11
12	13	14	15	16	17	18
19	20	21	22	23	24	25
26	27	28	29	30	31	

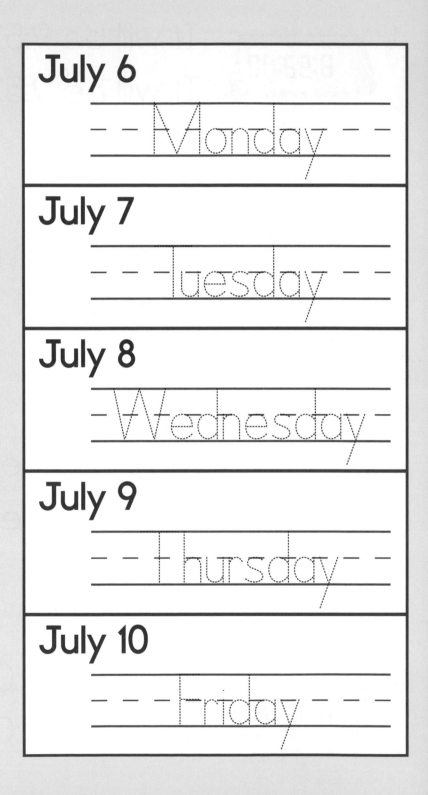

July 6

Monday

July 7

Tuesday

July 8

Wednesday

July 9

Thursday

July 10

Friday

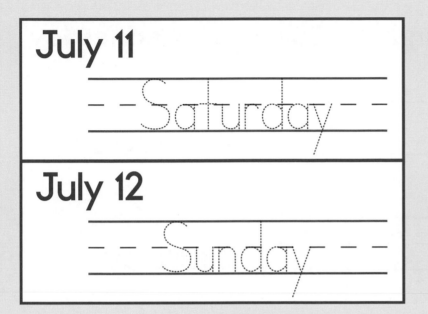

Weekdays = Monday, Tuesday, Wednesday, Thursday, Friday

Weekend = Saturday and Sunday

What day is today? _____

Days of the Week

Blank Out

FILL IN the blanks with the missing days of the week. CROSS OUT the words as you use them.

Friday   Monday   Sunday   Tuesday   Wednesday

Monday, _____ , Wednesday
1

Thursday, _____ , Saturday
2

Saturday, _____ , Monday
3

Tuesday, _____ , Thursday
4

Sunday, _____ , Tuesday
5

Criss Cross

WRITE the word for each clue in the grid.

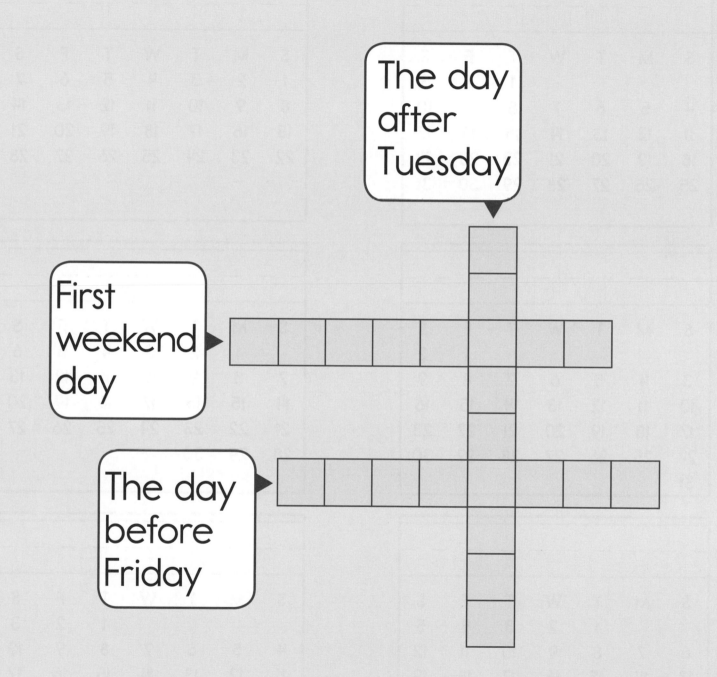

The day after Tuesday

First weekend day

The day before Friday

Months of the Year

Read and Trace

READ the words and TRACE them.

January

S	M	T	W	T	F	S
				1	2	3
4	5	6	7	8	9	10
11	12	13	14	15	16	17
18	19	20	21	22	23	24
25	26	27	28	29	30	31

February

S	M	T	W	T	F	S
1	2	3	4	5	6	7
8	9	10	11	12	13	14
15	16	17	18	19	20	21
22	23	24	25	26	27	28

May

S	M	T	W	T	F	S
					1	2
3	4	5	6	7	8	9
10	11	12	13	14	15	16
17	18	19	20	21	22	23
24	25	26	27	28	29	30
31						

June

S	M	T	W	T	F	S
	1	2	3	4	5	6
7	8	9	10	11	12	13
14	15	16	17	18	19	20
21	22	23	24	25	26	27
28	29	30				

September

S	M	T	W	T	F	S
		1	2	3	4	5
6	7	8	9	10	11	12
13	14	15	16	17	18	19
20	21	22	23	24	25	26
27	28	29	30			

October

S	M	T	W	T	F	S
					1	2	3
4	5	6	7	8	9	10
11	12	13	14	15	16	17
18	19	20	21	22	23	24
25	26	27	28	29	30	31

March

S	M	T	W	T	F	S
1	2	3	4	5	6	7
8	9	10	11	12	13	14
15	16	17	18	19	20	21
22	23	24	25	26	27	28
29	30	31				

April

S	M	T	W	T	F	S
			1	2	3	4
5	6	7	8	9	10	11
12	13	14	15	16	17	18
19	20	21	22	23	24	25
26	27	28	29	30		

July

S	M	T	W	T	F	S
			1	2	3	4
5	6	7	8	9	10	11
12	13	14	15	16	17	18
19	20	21	22	23	24	25
26	27	28	29	30	31	

August

S	M	T	W	T	F	S
						1
2	3	4	5	6	7	8
9	10	11	12	13	14	15
16	17	18	19	20	21	22
23	24	25	26	27	28	29
30	31					

November

S	M	T	W	T	F	S
1	2	3	4	5	6	7
8	9	10	11	12	13	14
15	16	17	18	19	20	21
22	23	24	25	26	27	28
29	30					

December

S	M	T	W	T	F	S
		1	2	3	4	5
6	7	8	9	10	11	12
13	14	15	16	17	18	19
20	21	22	23	24	25	26
27	28	29	30	31		

Months of the Year

Criss Cross

WRITE the word for each clue in the grid.

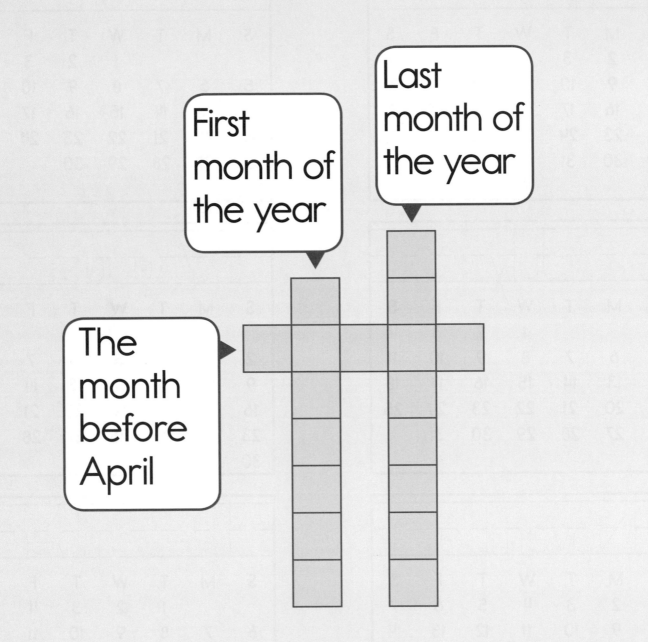

First month of the year

Last month of the year

The month before April

Blank Out

FILL IN the blanks with the missing months of the year. CROSS OUT the words as you use them.

August	February	January	May	November

January, _____ 1 , March

April, _____ 2 , June

July, _____ 3 , September

October, _____ 4 , December

December, _____ 5 , February

Read and Trace

READ the words and TRACE them. Do you know what they mean?

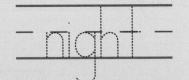

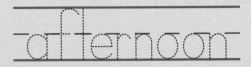

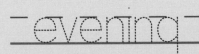

Criss Cross

WRITE the word for each clue in the grid.

Getting dark

Early in the day

Time for lunch

After dark

Blank Out

FINISH each sentence with a word from the word box. CROSS OUT the words as you use them.

morning   Noon   afternoon   evening   night

_____

_____ is when I eat lunch.
1

_____

When it is _____, I am in bed.
2

_____

The sun sets in the _____.
3

_____

I get out of bed in the _____.
4

_____

The baby naps in the _____.
5

Night and Day

DRAW a line to match each word under the moon to its opposite under the sun.

before   evening

night   after

early   late

light   day

morning   dark

Let's Eat!

Read and Trace

READ the words and TRACE them. Do you know what they mean?

meal

breakfast

lunch

snack

dinner

Match the Meaning

DRAW a line to match the meal with its time.

breakfast

lunch

snack

dinner

Let's Eat!

Blank Out!

FINISH each sentence with a word from the box. CROSS OUT the words as you use them.

breakfast   lunch   dinner   snack   meal

1. I wash my hands before every _____.

2. We eat _____ in the morning.

3. Noon is time for _____.

4. I eat a _____ between lunch and dinner.

5. We eat _____ in the evening.

Right or Wrong?

UNDERLINE the sentence that matches the picture.

1.

   It is time for dinner.

   It is time for lunch.

2. What a yummy snack!

   What a yummy dinner!

3. It is time for dinner.

   It is time for breakfast.

4. That's a big mail.

   That's a big meal.

Actions All Day Long

Read and Trace

READ the words and TRACE them.
Do you know what they mean?

To _wake_ is to stop sleeping and get out of bed.

To _start_ is to begin something.

To _finish_ is to end something .

To _hurry_ is to go fast. If you are late, you have to rush.

To _leave_ is to go out. Goodbye!

Match the Meaning

DRAW a line to match the words that have the **same** meaning..

start   get up

finish   begin

hurry   end

leave   go fast

wake   go

Actions All Day Long

Find the Friend

READ the clues. Then WRITE the friend's name under each picture.

Guy leaves the pool.

Yasmin finishes her dinner.

Ben starts a picture.

Tony wakes up.

_____

- - - - - - - - - -

_____

- - - - - - - - - -

_____

- - - - - - - - - -

_____

- - - - - - - - - -

Word Pictures

COLOR the spaces that show words for **actions**.

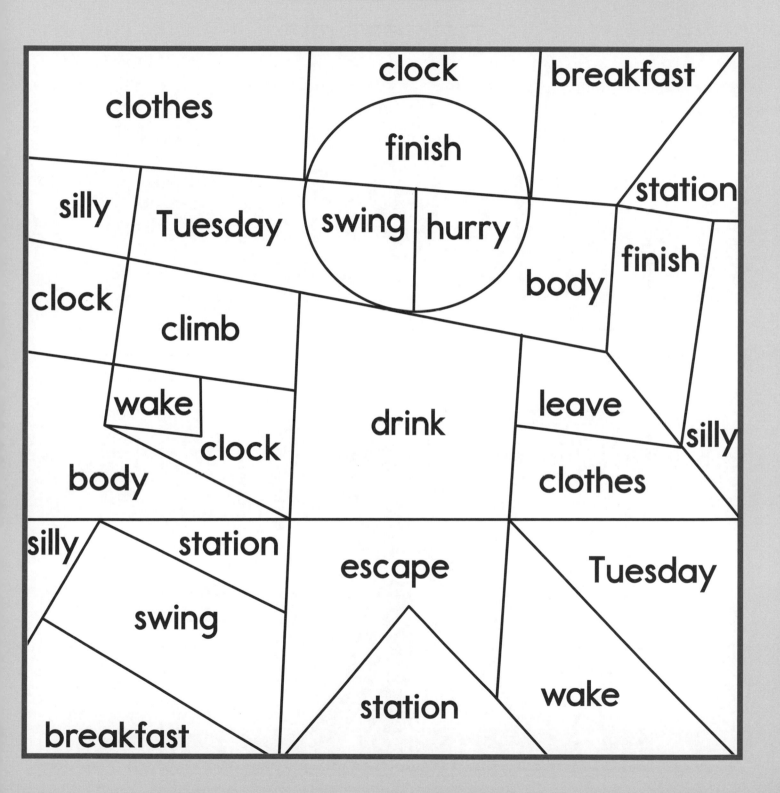

What's the Weather?

Read and Trace

READ the words and TRACE them. Do you know what they mean?

weather

rainy

sunny

cloudy

foggy

windy

Picture Pointers

WRITE the word for each picture clue in the grid.

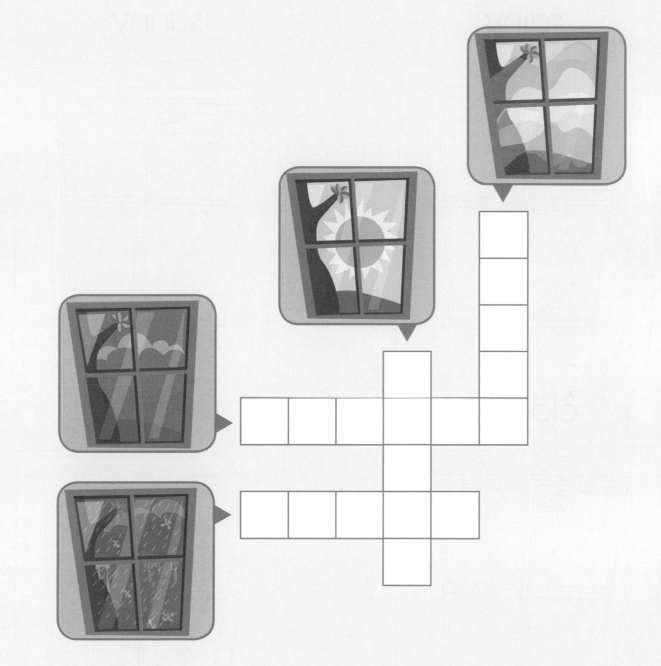

Draw It!

Help finish the pictures! Draw the pictures to match the words. Then COLOR the pictures.

rainy

sunny

cloudy

windy

Blank Out

FINISH each sentence with a word from the word box. CROSS OUT the words as you use them.

foggy	sunny	rainy	windy	weather

1. We will eat outside if the _____ is good.

2. It is hard to see far on a _____ day.

3. Your feet will get wet on a _____ day.

4. I hope it is hot and _____ on my birthday.

5. It was so _____, Marla's hat blew off!

Review

Blank Out

FILL IN the blanks with the missing months or days from the box. CROSS OUT the words as you use them.

February   Friday   July   October   Tuesday

January, _____ , March
1

Monday, _____ , Wednesday
2

June, _____ , August
3

Thursday, _____ , Saturday
4

September, _____ , November
5

Criss Cross

WRITE the word for each clue in the grid.

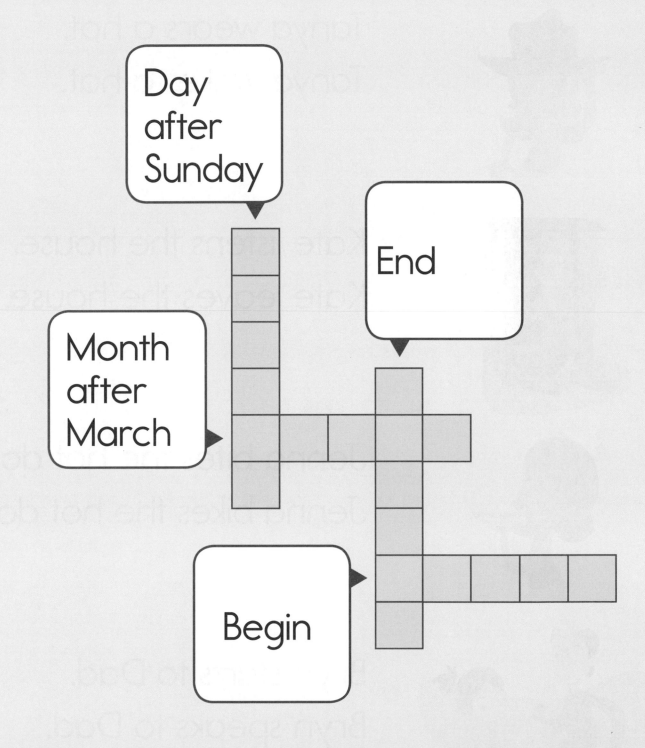

Day after Sunday

End

Month after March

Begin

Right or Wrong?

UNDERLINE the sentence that matches the picture.

1.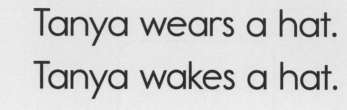

Tanya wears a hat.

Tanya wakes a hat.

2.

Kate listens the house.

Kate leaves the house.

3.

Jenna bites the hot dog.

Jenna bikes the hot dog.

4.

Bryn starts to Dad.

Bryn speaks to Dad.

across: on the other side of

action: something you do

afraid: scared

afternoon: the time between noon and evening

airplane:

angry: mad

April: the 4th month of the year

August: the 8th month of the year

balloon:

belong: when you have or own something, it's yours

below: under

beside: next to

between: in the middle

bike:

bite: chomp with your teeth

boat:

body:

bone:

breakfast: the first meal of the day

bridge:

building:

burglar:

button:

cage:

calendar:

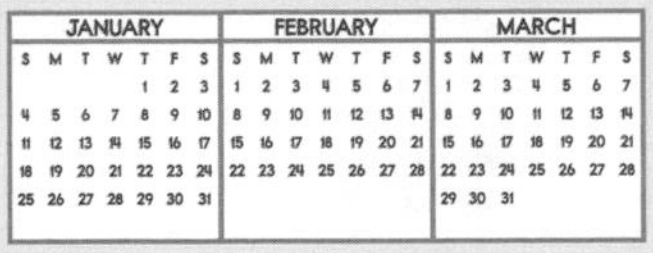

chase: to run after something or someone

climb: to go up, like on a ladder or in a tree

clock:

clothes:

cloudy:

coat:

colorful: having lots of colors, like a rainbow

cook: to make food hot on a stove or in an oven

dance: to move your body to music

date: the day of the year, like May 5, 2010

daughter: the girl child of a mother or father

December: the last month of the year

dinner: the last meal of the day

doctor:

drink: to swallow something liquid like milk or water

dry: the opposite of wet

escape: to run away or get out of a cage

evening: the time of day when it starts to get dark

family:

father: a man who has a child

February: the 2nd month of the year

finger:

finish: to end

float: to bob on top of the water

foggy:

fork:

Friday: the day of the week after Thursday

gorilla:

hers: belonging to her

hide: to go where no one can see you

his: belonging to him

hour: 60 minutes

hungry: needing to eat something

hurry: to rush, or go fast

inside: the opposite of outside

January: the 1st month of the year

jeans:

July: the 7th month of the year

June: the 6th month of the year

kangaroo:

kitchen:

knife:

leave: to go out

leopard:

listen: to hear

lunch: the meal you eat in the middle of the day

Index

mailman:

March: the 3rd month of the year

market:

May: the 5th month of the year

meal: food that you eat at a set time of day

mine: belonging to me

minute: part of an hour. There are 60 minutes in an hour.

Monday: the day of the week after Sunday

month: part of a year, like April. There are 12 months in a year.

morning: early in the day

mother: a woman who has a child

my: belonging to me

night: after dark

noon: 12 p.m.

nose:

November: the 11th month of the year

October: the 10th month of the year

ours: belonging to us

penguin:

pigeon:

playground:

policeman:

pool:

rainy:

Saturday: the day of the week after Friday

September: the 9th month of the year

sharp: pointy, something that can cut

shirt:

silly: funny, acting odd or crazy

skates:

snack: food you eat between meals

son: the boy child of a mother or father

speak: to say something

spoon:

start: to begin

station:

stove:

Sunday: the day of the week after Saturday

sunny:

swing: to move back and forth, like on a rope

taxi:

teacher: a person who shows others a lesson

teeth:

thirsty: dry, wanting to drink something

Thursday: the day of the week after Wednesday

Tuesday: the day of the week after Monday

unhappy: sad

visit: to go see a person or a place

wake: to stop sleeping and get up

walrus:

wash: to clean with soap and water

wear: to put clothes on your body

weather: what it's like outside—rainy, sunny, or cold

Wednesday: the day of the week after Tuesday

wheels:

windy:

year: 12 months, or 365 days

young: the opposite of old

yours: belonging to you

Answers

Page 211

```
      b
      o
      n
f i n g e r
      o
      s
      e
```

Page 212

Page 213

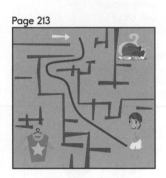

Page 215

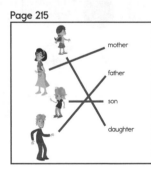

mother
father
son
daughter

Page 216

1. Mother hugs the baby.
2. Father and son eat.
3. This is a family.
4. The daughter is happy.

Page 217

Page 219

1. stove
2. knife
3. spoon
4. kitchen
5. fork

Page 220
Suggestions:

Page 221

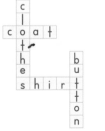

Page 223

```
c
c o a t
l
o      b
t      u
h s h i r t
e      t
s      o
       n
```

Page 224

Chuck
Tim
Ken
Pam

Page 225

Page 227

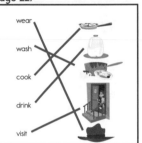

wear
wash
cook
drink
visit

Page 228

1. eat, run
2. play, wash
3. wear, hug
4. visit, cook

Page 229

1. I wash my hands.
2. I visit my granny.
3. I wear my mittens.
4. Bob drinks juice.

Page 231

unhappy
angry
afraid
happy

Page 232

1. sad, angry
2. afraid, happy
3. thirsty
4. hungry, mad

Page 233

afraid → scared
unhappy → sad
angry → mad
drink → sip
sleep → nap

Page 235

Page 236

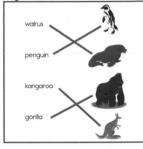

walrus
penguin
kangaroo
gorilla

Page 237

Page 239

1. YES
2. NO
3. NO
4. NO
5. YES

Answers

Page 240

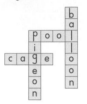

Page 241

Page 243
1. The balloon floats in the air.
2. I climb the tree.
3. The baby kangaroo is hiding.
4. The pigeon escapes.

Page 244
1. hide, see
2. drink, wear
3. swings, floats
4. escape, climb

Page 245

Page 247

Page 248
1. silly
2. sharp
3. colorful
4. dry
5. young

Page 249
wet → dry
unhappy → happy
hot → cold
young → old
gray → colorful

Page 252
1. mine
2. his
3. yours
4. her
5. ours

Page 253
Lori → Lori's
me → mine
you → yours
him → his
her → hers
us → ours

Page 255

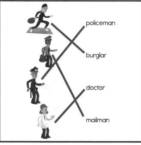

Page 256
1. people
2. doctor
3. mailman
4. teacher
5. policeman

Page 257

Page 259

Page 260
1. Jamal is in the building.
2. Katya is on the bridge.
3. The bus is at the station.
4. Dad goes to the market.

Page 261

Page 263

Page 264

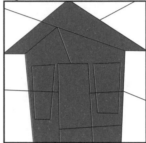

Page 265

Page 267
1. listen
2. speak
3. chase
4. dance
5. bite

Page 268
1. wear, visit
2. swing, escape
3. bite, chase
4. listen, dance

Page 269
1. The dog bites the bone.
2. I speak on the phone.
3. Rudy chases the ball.
4. Bella dances on the rug.

Page 271

Page 272
wet → dry
below → over
inside → outside
mine → yours
dance → sit

Page 273

Answers

Page 276
1. clock
2. hour
3. month
4. calendar
5. year

Page 277
1. It will be 9:52 in one hour.
2. Next year it will be 2012.
3. May 15 is the date of the party.
4. It will be 10:05 in five minutes.

Page 280
1. Tuesday
2. Friday
3. Sunday
4. Wednesday
5. Monday

Page 281

Page 284
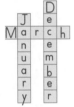

Page 285
1. February
2. May
3. August
4. November
5. January

Page 287

Page 288
1. Noon
2. night
3. evening
4. morning
5. afternoon

Page 289
before → after
night → day
early → late
light → dark
morning → evening

Page 291
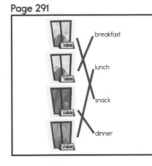

Page 292
1. meal
2. breakfast
3. lunch
4. snack
5. dinner

Page 293
1. It is time for lunch.
2. What a yummy snack!
3. It is time for dinner.
4. That's a big meal.

Page 295
start → begin
finish → end
hurry → go fast
leave → go
wake → get up

Page 296

Page 297

Page 299

Page 300

Page 301
1. weather
2. foggy
3. rainy
4. sunny
5. windy

Page 302
1. February
2. Tuesday
3. July
4. Friday
5. October

Page 303

Page 304
1. Tanya wears a hat.
2. Kate leaves the house.
3. Jenna bites the hot dog.
4. Bryn speaks to Dad.